Tolerance

TOWARD A NEW CIVILITY

Glenn Tinder

UNIVERSITY OF MASSACHUSETTS PRESS
AMHERST 1976

Publication of this book was assisted by the
American Council of Learned Societies under a grant
from the Andrew W. Mellon Foundation.

Library of Congress Cataloging in Publication Data

Tinder, Glenn E
    Tolerance : toward a new civility.
    Includes bibliographical references and index.
    1. Liberty of speech.   2. Toleration.   I. Title.
JC591.T55 1976   323.44'3   75-8453
ISBN 0-87023-186-3

CONTENTS

To Gloria, Galen and Evan

ACKNOWLEDGMENTS

I would like to thank three people who helped me to bring this book to completion: Gloria Tinder, my wife, who not only typed the manuscript but sustained me with a patience and interest that never failed; Galen Tinder, my older son, who for several years has given me intelligent and sympathetic support in my thinking and writing; and finally Jack Beatty, former student and close friend, who went over the manuscript in its entirety, making valuable suggestions concerning both style and content, and who has also provided intellectual companionship of a kind that is rare and priceless in our distracted times.

Attentiveness is the rarest and purest form of generosity.
Simone Weil

Introduction

LET ME DEFINE our subject at the outset. These reflections are concerned not merely with freedom of religion but with freedom of communication in general. My interest in this broader concept is indicated by my use of the word "tolerance," as distinguished from "toleration," which is often defined in terms of religious freedom. In Webster's Second Edition, for example, toleration is defined as the "policy of permitting the existence of all (or given) religious opinions and modes of worship contrary to, or different from, those of the established church or belief." Tolerance, in the same dictionary, is defined without particular reference to religion; it is "the disposition to tolerate beliefs, practices, or habits differing from one's own." It is tolerance, the broader attitude, to which we address ourselves in the following pages.

One other comment defining the subject of these reflections seems in order. I shall deal primarily with tolerance of expression as distinguished from tolerance of action, and, for the sake of convenience, will ordinarily use the word "tolerance" (exceptions will be obvious from the context) to mean "tolerance of expression." Of course action is often, and perhaps even usually, a form of expression. But there is a difference between expression and what might be called "pure action." Through expression, one tries to enable another person to see things from one's own viewpoint; hence the other is treated as a being like oneself (in terms popularized by existentialist writings, the other is treated as a "subject" and what is aimed at is "intersubjectivity"). Through "pure action," on the other hand, one aims at altering an outward condition without affecting the minds of others. Delivering a speech, then, is expression and repairing an automobile engine is pure action. There is, of course, a large area in between, constituted largely of efforts to alter outward conditions through affecting the minds of others; advertising exemplifies this middle area. Is advertising to be classified as expression or as action? I do not think that it is necessary to try to decide, because I am not trying here to settle a question bearing decisively on my argument or even to delimit the subject matter in a way that determines method or approach. I am only pointing out to the reader the general area that will be explored.

The two main boundary lines of that area, in summary, are "tolerance" and "expression." This essay is a rethinking of the freedom to communicate.

Such a rethinking is necessary in part because tolerance is being widely and forcibly attacked—which perhaps is natural, for, as I will try to show, tolerance is not easily achieved and is not likely ever to be wholly secure and uncontroversial. Many radicals believe that tolerance is supported by dominant groups because, although purportedly it exposes them to criticism, in fact it helps to keep them in power. According to typical radical criticism, while anyone may say whatever he pleases, the deficiencies and injustices of the established society are rarely brought fully to light. In a variety of ways, many so subtle and apparently immutable that most people never notice them, social criticism is discouraged and nullified. From this point of view, tolerance may seem to be worse than useless, for those who might in other circumstances attack the injustices around them are lulled into an indecisive open-mindedness. They unconsciously resign themselves to a realm of free public expression which, like a quarantine ward in a hospital, is maintained in sterilized separateness from the rest of the society. Tolerance thus means, above all, tolerance of injustice. Today many unselfish and well-educated people, particularly among the young, believe that those who wish to change society radically are apt to waste their time if they enter into discussion with conservative opponents. The results of this attitude have been seen in the shouting down of unpopular speakers, in the violent interruption of regular activities in universities, and in the destruction of property and occasionally even of life.

On the opposite side of the political spectrum, dominant groups and those of conservative convictions have in one sense been more respectful of speech and other forms of expression: they have been afraid of them. Unlike the radicals, they have seemed to feel that in some circumstances, at least, the established order is imperiled by tolerance. Thus, as the war in Vietnam became increasingly unpopular, the government in Washington mounted a campaign designed to curb criticism and to discredit the opposition, and in their references to radicals in the universities officials indulged in obloquy so pronounced and persistent that it could only be understood as a deliberate refusal to engage in reasoned discourse.

Particular perils to tolerance may, of course, quickly pass. Their importance lies not so much in their immediate consequences (for tolerance has often been threatened before and has survived) as in the enduring situation they reveal, for modern man is involved in difficulties so numerous and perplexing that it is tempting to despair of the human race. Such problems as urban disintegration, the pollution of air and water, overpopulation, racial hatred, and war seem certain, even if all goes as well as we can reasonably hope, sorely to vex and burden governments and to fill with tension the lives of ordinary citizens for several generations to come. This is a bleak prospect for tolerance. Not only is it hard for men to put up with the challenge of unrestricted expression when they are confused and frightened; but even to cold, non-partisan reason the troubles that surround us may seem to require dictatorial, and thus intolerant, measures. This is why recent attacks on tolerance must be taken with utmost seriousness even though they may be ephemeral and, by themselves, inconsequential; they are signs that we have entered a time that will be highly unfavorable to tolerance.

Rethinking tolerance may help us to remember the reasons for being tolerant. We must guard against accepting the notion that political goals can be reached only by shouting down (if not by shooting down) one's opponents. Reflecting on tolerance may be one way of doing so.

But there is a further necessity for undertaking the task set by this essay. Attacks on tolerance do not merely challenge us to recall certain obviously valid reasons, long known, why people should allow one another freedom of expression. Tolerance is surprisingly hard to defend, and anyone who tries to do so is likely to find that the problem is not merely to *recall* its grounds but to *discover* them.

Why should tolerance be so hard to defend? The answer is that it means allowing publicity, and a chance of victory, to thoughts you despise. To be tolerant is to grant those whose beliefs you think endanger peace, or justice, or some other great common good, the right to try to win others over to their beliefs. Why should one gratuitously grant such an advantage to one's opponents? Most people shrug off this question (at least when it is only theoretically presented to them) with some such remark as, "Who am I to say what endangers the common good? Perhaps beliefs I reject are nevertheless true." Of course it is undeniable that any particular person may be mistaken, and in running society it seems sensible to take this into account by letting a number of persons have a say.

This, however, is to look at things from the outside. To look at them them from the inside, by trying to live the attitude expressed in the above remark, will quickly make it apparent that tolerance is not just a matter of elementary common sense. "Who am I to say . . . ?" The answer is that every responsible person has to say what he considers necessary for, and dangerous to, peace, justice, and other values. He cannot do this without believing that he himself is right and that those who greatly differ from him are wrong. It is in accord not only with human nature, but also with the logic of having convictions to wish in some fashion to silence those who disagree. If we are really to face this issue, it is not enough to ponder it in abstraction from the realities and problems around us; we must think of actual persons whose outlook seems alien and whose influence we fear. A liberal or radical, for example, must call to mind particular conservatives or reactionaries with whose views he deeply disagrees and then ask himself why he should be willing to arrange things so that those views have a chance of being heard and of winning a majority to their side. A conservative must subject himself to a like examination with respect to opinions and social movements he despises. Those who honestly test themselves in this way are apt to discover reservations and uncertainties they had not expected to find.

In America, tolerance has for many generations been firmly established both as law, being a requirement of the First Amendment to the Constitution, and as morality, as part of the political creed that almost everyone professes (though does not always follow). Thus it is easy for us to think of tolerance as altogether natural and logical and to assume that several fully adequate and self-evident reasons for being tolerant could readily be found by anyone who took the trouble to look for them. In this way we forget what was widely realized three hundred years ago, before tolerance was established, that tolerance is in some respects unnatural and illogical.

The most cursory glance at history indicates that this is so. If tolerance were wholly natural and logical, presumably it would generally have prevailed throughout history, and periods of intolerance would have been exceptional. But such, of course, is not the case. So far as it is possible to generalize about so complex a matter (there have never been societies either tolerant of everything or tolerant of nothing, although a few have approached either extreme), it is probably valid to say that intolerance has been normal and tolerance exceptional. For Christian Europe, from roughly the fourth to the seventeenth century, tolerance toward all persons and all beliefs was not an idea to be seriously considered. Not that all variations in thought and worship were suppressed; but it was everywhere assumed that it was the duty of society and government to support a single, authoritatively formulated faith, and thus the idea of tolerance, in anything like its modern form, could hardly even arise. Ancient Greeks and Romans were more tolerant than medieval Christians. Their tolerance was highly imperfect, however, as is suggested by examples familiar to everyone: the execution of Socrates by the Athenians and the slaughter of Christians by the Romans. And not only was ancient pagan tolerance imperfect; it was also, it might be said, incidental. It was practiced because it was convenient, or even inevitable, in view of the prevailing varieties of thought and belief and the fact that the techniques and instruments of totalitarian control had not as yet been developed; but tolerance was not thought of as a chief characteristic of a good society. The values aimed at were rather justice, peace, and virtue.

Only during the last two or three hundred years, and in but a few societies, has freedom of expression been ranked among the principal ends of social existence. Further, the tolerance that has actually been achieved has been precarious and has suffered recurrent attacks; hence the poverty and ostracism that plagued most of the great French painters of the nineteenth century and the annihilation of freedom that accompanied the rise of Fascist and Nazi totalitarianism.

Surely, intolerance would not have been so powerful throughout history if every good argument had been against it. We should remember that for the most part intolerance has been practiced by people who felt morally bound to be intolerant. People have usually been intolerant not because they defected from their principles but because they adhered to them. Defending tolerance thus is not merely a matter of calling to mind a few propositions so obviously true that no reasonable person could dispute them. It may well be that, as a value, tolerance is more open to doubt than is peace, economic security for everyone, or any other widely accepted ideal of our time.

It is not surprising, therefore, that the traditional arguments in favor of tolerance, set forth in certain classical philosophical treatises later to be discussed, are weak. It seems likely that tolerance finally became established less because the philosophical case for it seemed overwhelming than because the destructiveness of the religious wars, the apparently irrepressible character of religious differences, and a growing secularism made it seem sensible. It did not need the support of an argument grounded in philosophical first-principles. Also, these classical statements were framed by Englishmen and addressed primarily to their fellow countrymen, and English thought has long shown a bias toward practicality and common sense. Thus both circumstances and audience permitted the case for tolerance to be made in a way that was less than philosophically searching. Since it was not inherently (that is, aside from propitious circumstances) an easy case to make, the upshot was that the arguments we have inherited are somewhat makeshift. To most of us they still seem at first glance reasonable, but as soon as one reflects on them their fragility becomes apparent.

Thus tolerance is weak not only as an institution but also as a theory; to rethink tolerance involves more than recollection—it involves new construction.

It is important for us to succeed in this task. Common sense seemed to serve fairly well while tolerance was convenient. But now that we seem to be entering a time when order around us, and assurance within, recurrently come near to collapsing, we may find common sense revising its counsel. This would not be surprising if tolerance is really as paradoxical as I have suggested. Its survival may depend on an appreciation that will cause us to practice tolerance even when it is troublesome and painful to do so. It is doubtful that common sense alone can impose that kind of discipline.

I do not offer this essay as *the* rethinking that is needed. It is only *a* rethinking, and it has been carried on in the hope that it will be useful in suggesting directions and exploring uncharted terrain. I believe that the formulation of a new philosophy of tolerance will depend on epistemological analysis of a kind I am not competent to undertake; and it will almost certainly require the work of several thinkers.

The present reflections have three specific purposes subordinate to their over-all exploratory purpose. At the outset, I wish to show the weaknesses of the traditional arguments, and to trace these arguments back to premises which seemed indisputable to the liberal thinkers who created the ideal of tolerance but extremely dubious to many later minds.

The second aim of the essay is to adopt a new set of premises that will be more nearly in accord with contemporary attitudes and and to see whether tolerance is still defensible on these new grounds. I shall argue that it is. The result, however, will not be merely to put new foundations under the old ideal. With the new foundations the ideal itself will change, and the core of this essay will emerge—a tentative sketch of a new concept of tolerance.

Finally, I shall try to draw out the implications of this new concept for human relations in general and political order in particular. My intention in doing this will be not only to clarify the nature of tolerance but also to suggest that in understanding tolerance we solve more than one problem. We gain a foothold that may help us to hang on against the gales of fanaticism and despair that are sweeping over us and from which in time it may be possible to ascend to a new political wisdom and a new political poise. I shall try to show that authentic tolerance is a large part of civility—of the capacity for sharing existence.

At this point a few procedural comments are required. As stated above, I begin with what I have been calling "the traditional arguments." How are these to be defined? There is a danger in being so subjective that the arguments criticized constitute only "straw men," to be deliberately rendered vulnerable to the destruction I wish to inflict on them. In order to minimize this danger (which I do not think can be wholly eliminated), I take as the two classical statements of the idea of tolerance John Locke's *Letter Concerning Toleration* (1685) and John Stuart Mill's *On Liberty* (1859). By letting Locke and Mill speak for tolerance, I hope to curb my own natural inclination to make the traditional arguments look weaker than they really are.

In basing my argument on these two texts, however, I encounter two other problems to which brief reference must be made. The first of these is that Locke's immediate concern was a good deal narrower than Mill's, or than that of the present essay. Locke wrote about toleration, not tolerance; further, he confined his attention to the question of why governments, rather than the populace as a whole (Mill was particularly concerned with the attitudes of society generally), should be tolerant. It seems to me, however, that it would be pedantic to ignore the fact that in arguing for toleration on the part of governments Locke was opening up the whole field of tolerance. Mill acknowledged this when he wrote, of religious conflict, that it has been "on this battlefield, almost solely, that the rights of the individual against society have been asserted on broad grounds of principle, and the claim of society to exercise authority over dissentients openly controverted." [1] In giving philosophical support to religious freedom, Locke in effect was helping to introduce the case for freedom of expression generally. Accordingly, the principles on which Locke based his defense of toleration on the part of governments became prominent among those on which a broader idea came to rest: that all kinds of expression should be permitted, and not only by governments but by every power in society. This is why I ignore (although I hope cautiously enough so that Locke is not misconstrued) the fact that Locke's subject was somewhat narrower than the subject of this essay.

The second problem involved in treating Locke and Mill as classical exponents of traditional liberal views is that neither thinker can be accurately regarded as a pure type. A great mind can never be fully characterized in terms of an established ideological classification. Accordingly, neither Locke nor Mill is a classical liberal and nothing more. Neither was blind to the values expressed in other political philosophies nor failed to introduce hints of those values into his own writing. Indeed, Mill, whose intellectual sympathies and intuitions far outran his own powers of theoretical organization, foreshadows in many passages the outlook I shall try to sketch in this essay.

So far as I ignore qualities not in conformity with the classical liberalism I am analyzing, my excuse is partly methodological—that thus our own thinking can more readily advance—and partly that in a sense Locke and Mill did so themselves. They did not consciously transcend their basic liberal principles. This is particularly true of Mill, who never fully recognized the positions toward which his mind had spontaneously moved; insights of originality and importance were never embodied in philosophical principles and related systematically with the rest of his thinking. Hence, while his reflections on tolerance often carried him away from traditional views, he remained very explicitly committed to those views.

By concentrating on the liberal elements in the thought of Locke and Mill, however, I do not wish to make those thinkers appear to be more vulnerable than they really are or to make it seem that I am engaged in an undertaking so ambitious and dubious as that of attacking all of their ideas and setting up others in their place. Locke and Mill seem to me to be thinkers of permanent worth, and I regard the essay *On Liberty* as among the best works on politics ever written. But the thinking of both men was encumbered, I believe, by liberal preconceptions; in both, understanding was superior to explicit theoretical form. What I am trying to do, then, is in a sense to extract valid insights from the doctrines encasing them.

Let us now examine those doctrines.

I Tolerance and the Liberal Faith

WE SHALL BEGIN with the explicit arguments of Locke and of Mill; after these have been discussed the philosophical premises underlying them will be considered. This discussion focuses on six basic arguments, which in turn are organized under three headings—the relationship of the individual and society, the nature of belief and truth, and the probability of historical progress. It is well to note that neither Locke nor Mill organized his arguments in this way; moreover, other readers might formulate and group the various arguments somewhat differently than I have. However, while the discussion has thus been organized with a view to convenience of exposition and analysis, I think the substance fairly represents the dominant ideas of Locke and Mill concerning tolerance.

Further, I believe that this substance represents the views not only of two men but of an old and powerful tradition—that of liberalism. The idea of tolerance has been shaped by the liberal faith. The six arguments to be considered would be acceptable, I think, not only to Locke and Mill but to most liberals of the past two or three hundred years. When the philosophical premises of these arguments are defined, they will be seen to constitute a general statement of the liberal philosophy. And when I suggest a different theory of tolerance in the following chapter, I will be trying to render a liberal ideal I believe to be of universal worth independent of liberal premises that to me and to many others seem to have become untenable.

The first two arguments concern human relations.

THE TRADITIONAL ARGUMENTS: THE INDIVIDUAL AND SOCIETY

1

If there is one idea that Locke and Mill more frequently cite and more highly esteem than any other, it is their concept of the supreme value of the autonomous and unique individual. To say that the individual is autonomous is to say that he makes up his own mind; his beliefs represent his own judgments and his actions represent his own decisions. Locke is expressing the ideal of autonomy when he writes, "The care . . . of every man's soul belongs unto himself, and is to be left unto himself." [1] In matters bearing on salvation, he asserts, "Every man . . . has the supreme and absolute authority of judging for himself." [2] Mill's thought, and even his words, are remarkably close to Locke's. "The only freedom which deserves the name," he writes, "is that of pursuing our own good in our own way . . . Each is the proper guardian of his own health, whether bodily, *or* mental and spiritual." [3]

As for uniqueness, Locke would never admit that "strait is the gate, and narrow is the way, which leadeth unto life." [4] If uniqueness does not in itself give one a claim to eternal glory, it certainly does not bar such a claim. "Why am I beaten and ill-used by others," Locke asks, "because, perhaps, I wear not buskins; because my hair is not of the right cut; . . . because I avoid certain by-ways, which seem unto me to lead into briars or precipices; . . . because I avoid to keep company with some travelers that are less grave, and others that are more sour than they ought to be?" [5] In Mill's essay it is easy for the reader to feel that uniqueness has become eternal glory in itself; the blessed and redeemed, in Mill's vision, are those with the gifts and the courage to become unlike anyone else. Mill has been plausibly charged with celebrating mere eccentricity, and his essay is the progenitor of a multitude of writings that denounce "conformity" and call on each man to develop his own unique beliefs, tastes, and habits.

What objection is there to arguing for tolerance on these grounds? As the uniformities induced by mass production, by centralized media of communication, and by other forces in twentieth-century industrial society have spread and been more widely recognized, many have come to share Mill's feeling that the primary requirement for being human is to be different. Is not one's very selfhood lost once one has become indistinguishable from multitudes of other human beings?

It is clearly impossible to reject totally the ideal of the autonomous and unique individual. Today, it takes neither a very macabre nor a very powerful imagination to conceive of a society not far in the future when behavioristic learning, industrial and organizational skill, and dictatorial ambition will combine to turn men into masses of living mechanisms, all alike and all under the perfect control of supreme managers. Although such a society probably could not be actually established, it is a fantasy that epitomizes several strong contemporary trends; and in recoiling from these we feel that what is endangered is a value, often referred to as our "humanity," that is not merely one value among others, to be trimmed and adjusted in order to fit into a whole range of values making up the good life, but a ground without which there can be no other values and no good life ("What shall a man give in exchange for his soul?"). The value of the autonomous individual cannot be casually criticized or dismissed.

It will be one of my aims in the following chapter to restate and save what is valid in their ideal. What has to be done here is to try to see what is erroneous in it. This can best be done, I think, by looking at the ideal of uniqueness.

Locke and Mill take little account of the similarity that binds every individual to his society. This similarity is both inevitable and willed. It would be tedious to devote very much attention to all of the conditions rendering similarity among members of the same society inevitable. Some of the main configurations of one's personality are created during infancy and early childhood, before one has the capacity consciously to choose; one is educated with many others in schools that would not be viable were they not representative of the surrounding society; the lives that serve as models must be found mainly in one's own society; one must work, find companions, and enjoy recreation within his own society. These familiar necessities all tend to produce uniformity.

A more novel way of calling attention to the inevitability of similarity among members of the same society is to note that an individual can perceive and handle reality only by means of the mental framework his society provides. In all thinking and deciding, one is guided by assumptions, for the most part unconscious, as to what is good, what can be taken as true without being demonstrated, what constitutes adequate proof, and so forth. We cannot view reality without a framework made up of such assumptions, except perhaps in rare and evanescent glimpses; nor does the individual have creative power enough to devise a framework of his own. On the whole, we see what society enables us to see. One can alter his mental framework so that it accords with his own temperament and situation; but in doing so one is almost certain to employ the standards—that is, the components of a mental framework—which society has provided him. Although this dependence may not be an appealing condition, I suggest that it is inescapable and that social thought cannot begin to understand such ideals as liberty and individuality until the fated similarity affecting every person has been taken into account.

The general point, of course, is commonplace in the context of contemporary social thought and research. Almost every sociological and historical work, offering generalizations about society that can hold only because of the similarities uniting multitudes of individuals, gives them support.

The reader may object that to speak thus is to take account only of the thoughtless and conformist crowd and not of those who are creative. But it is perhaps the creative few who have provided the most striking evidence that similarity is inevitable. Art, philosophy, literature, and all other forms of creative expression reflect cultural—usually national—styles. A great painter like Henri Matisse produced hundreds of works of art, and most of them are thoroughly and obviously French; an original thinker, Karl Jaspers, expresses his Kantian and Hegelian background in all of his major works; Dostoevsky and Tolstoy, who have seemed to some readers so different as to constitute two distinct and primary spiritual types, stand out as typical nineteenth-century Russian minds when compared with Faulkner or Joyce. The rule of similarity seems to hold, moreover, not only for artistic, philosophical, and literary genius, but even for those who have set directions for history. Was not Socrates emphatically Greek and Jesus fundamentally Hebraic?

But does not historical development require a large measure of individual uniqueness through which established patterns are altered and new directions suggested? Further, how can a person possess his own reality and dignity unless he is definitely different from every other person? Answering these questions, I suspect, depends on recognizing that the historical role and value of individual persons cannot be determined by an objective scale such as one running from "similarity" at one extreme to "uniqueness" at the other, a possibility that will be explored in the following chapter. My purpose here in asking these questions is only to point out that there are mysteries involved in the issue we are considering; I am not trying to dissipate these mysteries by invoking the concept of similarity as against that of uniqueness. But it does seem that Locke and Mill, and others as well, in falling into the habit of celebrating uniqueness have largely ignored national and cultural similarities so compelling as to throw their ideal into question.

Nor is similarity merely a fate; it is also a value. To begin with, according to an outlook so widespread and enduring that it might be considered as perennial moral wisdom, man is subject to standards that are universal—the same for all. The ideal man would thus, in achieving excellence, become similar—not to all others, but to all who are excellent. Friedrich Nietzsche rebelled against this moral outlook, and he has been followed by other thinkers, even by Christians such as Nicolai Berdyaev. Through this rebellion, moral nobility has come to be viewed by many more as a matter of creativity than as mere obedience to rules—undoubtedly an advance. Still, it remains very difficult to envision moral effort and achievement strictly in terms of uniqueness. A good man is presumably not entirely indescribable and incomprehensible; but if he can be described and understood in terms of such qualities as compassion and courage, then he embodies universals; finally, if these universals make up part of our definition of goodness, so that we would not, for example, call a man 'good' if he were lacking in compassion or in courage, then all good men are in certain crucial ways similar.

Similarity seems to be a value in another respect. According to much of the social philosophy and scholarly work of recent times, one of the strongest human impulses is to join with others. Sociological studies bring out the bewilderment and pain caused by alienation; psychologists argue that loving and being loved are indispensable to mental health. Social philosophers seem increasingly inclined, since the time of Rousseau, to interpret man as a communal being. But one cannot join with others unless he becomes like them in some respects. While community does not require the obliteration of all differences, it does depend on numerous similarities—on common experiences, common interests, and so forth. Thus, if it is man's nature to seek community, it is his nature also to seek similarity.

Finally, it seems that it is only through similarity, rather than uniqueness, that man can establish an adequate relationship with the human past. An indispensable bond in such a relationship is tradition; merely to possess historical knowledge, without participating in a tradition, places one in a position of rational detachment. The end, however, is not to dwell within the past. It is rather to effect continuity between the past and one's own life, to avoid, in part, the proud and ridiculous project of starting out altogether anew, as though earlier generations had gained no experience and made no discoveries. The purpose of seeking continuity is also to take part in the affairs of the human race, even in defiance of the passage of generations. Such are the main grounds for giving care and respect to tradition. Tradition, however, is common. Hence one's responsibility and regard for it can only be expressed through striving to share with others its beliefs and customs, that is, through striving for similarity.

The notion that one aspect of moral effort is a striving for certain kinds of similarity summarizes some of the main deficiencies I have pointed to in the ideal of uniqueness. No doubt existence as a person entails being different in some ways from all other persons; but it also surely entails trying to participate in the universally human, in the common, and in the traditional. There is something seriously wrong with a concept of individuality that obscures and depreciates this essential aspect of human existence.

Aside from neglecting the claims of similarity, liberal doctrine is misleading in implying that there is an objective index of personal being. The very emphasis that Mill placed on uniqueness—an observable characteristic, involving comparisons between one person and another, and thus involving reason—testifies to a more or less impersonalist mode of thought. Kierkegaard, the primary originator of the personalism represented by the existentialist and phenomenological movements in philosophy, spoke quite definitely on this matter: an authentic Christian, who for Kierkegaard necessarily realized his personal being with the utmost possible intensity, would be outwardly indistinguishable from everyone else. Personal being was achieved and manifested inwardly. We shall return to this theme later on in this essay.

Little has been said in this argument about the ideal of autonomy as distinguished from uniqueness. This is in part because the ideal of autonomy in its most general form does not seem to me deserving of criticism; I would not want to begin an essay in political thought by questioning the importance of choice. Aside from this, in the more specific form it assumed in the thought of Mill, and perhaps of Locke as well, autonomy was so indistinguishably joined with uniqueness that criticisms of the latter apply to the former as well. Mill conceived of autonomy not only as the capacity for choice but also as the capacity for choosing a unique and separate individual existence. It is doubtful that deliberately choosing similarity and community would have struck Mill as exemplifying autonomy.

It is to be remembered in connection with this initial chapter

that my intention is to point out serious weaknesses in the traditional conception of tolerance but not to reject it totally. In the
next chapter, an attempt will be made to reformulate the truth
represented, however inadequately, by the ideals of autonomy
and uniqueness. The theme of the present argument is relatively
restricted: if, instead of being the supreme value it tended to be in
Mill's essay, uniqueness is seen as limited both in feasibility and
desirability, the tolerance that is justified on the grounds that it
makes uniqueness possible suffers a corresponding loss in value.

Among the traditional arguments, there is another that also
makes a sharp separation between individual and society.

2

Both Locke and Mill argue that the individual occupies a sphere of
life defined not by law but by the very nature of society, within
which he can think and act with little or no effect on others. Thus
Locke asserted that "one man does not violate the right of another
by his erroneous opinions and undue manner of worship," [6] and
Mill provided the strongest and most famous statement of the
idea—a statement on which he based his entire essay—when he
wrote that "there is a sphere of action in which society, as distinguished from the individual, has, if any, only an indirect interest;
comprehending all that portion of a person's life and conduct
which affects only himself, or if it also affects others, only with
their free, voluntary, and undeceived consent and participation." [7]

What follows with strict logical necessity from this idea is not
that tolerance is good but that, so far as the interests of society
are concerned, there can be no sound, practical objection to it. Any
thoughts and actions that have no appreciable bearing on the welfare of others might as well be left wholly to the discretion of the
one whose thoughts and actions they are. If these constitute a
large sphere of life, as Mill believed, then much may be tolerated.
Although this argument, strictly construed, concerns only the feasibility of tolerance, it readily takes on a moral coloring. It can easily be said that thoughts and actions not affecting anyone else are
not the proper business of anyone else. The disjunction between
individual and society that is held to be natural, merely in the
sense of being the way things are, easily comes to be treated as natural in the sense of being morally obligatory. This tendency, it has
often been pointed out, is particularly marked in Mill, who, as a

utilitarian, was ostensibly opposed to the old idea of natural law—
of a moral law deriving from the nature of man and society. But
to him, that "sphere of action in which society . . . has, if any,
only an indirect interest" became in effect a sphere of rights be-
stowed by natural law.

The principal weakness in this argument is, I think, manifest to
most people today, owing partly perhaps to the influence of the
many social thinkers and sociologists who have decisively departed
from Mill's outlook. What Mill referred to as "that portion of a
person's life and conduct which affects only himself" is so small
and insignificant that it cannot make up a sphere of liberty worth
caring about. A society tolerating only that segment of an individual's life and thought that (using another phrase of Mill's) "merely concerns himself," would be suffocatingly intolerant. [8] It is quite
true that Mill did not hold that self-regarding acts *alone* should be
tolerated and all else regulated; certain acts affecting others might
be allowed to fall within the sphere of liberty. But Mill was willing
to leave that to the circumstances of the moment and the discretion of authorities; the extent of inviolable liberty was defined
wholly in terms of the distinction between acts concerning primarily oneself and acts concerning others. And here he certainly placed
himself in a weak theoretical position. Society can be more accurately envisioned as a tightly woven net in which the tearing of one
strand is apt to loosen others than as a honeycomb in which each
man can occupy his own cell in isolation. Anything that very much
concerns one individual, such as illness or loss of work, must at
least concern members of his family and fellow workers as well. If
he is a leader or teacher, or in some other way has wide influence
or connections, then many others will be involved in his affairs.
One person's concerns are never purely his own but must always
affect the welfare of others.

Moreover, people presumably care for one another, or a least
ought to, in a way that is not merely selfish. A second criticism that
can be directed against the argument that we should be tolerant because a significant portion of an individual's behavior affects no
one but himself is that, so far as it takes on the moral coloring referred to above, asserting not merely the feasibility but the moral
obligation of ignoring such "self-regarding" behavior, the argument
is inhumane. It tells us that we should be indifferent to others except where they threaten our interests. In Locke, this weakness in

the traditional position is strikingly clear. It must be remembered that Locke was an avowed Christian. In view of the acute sense of responsibility Christians have from the beginning evinced toward men generally, particularly in matters deemed to bear on their prospects of salvation, it is startling to be told by Locke that one man's "perdition" is no "prejudice to another man's affairs." [9] At another point, Locke assures the reader that "if any man err from the right way, it is his own misfortune, no injury to thee." [10] It is true that Locke is trying here to distinguish and separate the civil and religious realms, and most of us, including the author of this essay, very much approve of this effort. What concerns us, however, is only that Locke (and Mill after him, although less explicitly), in trying to defend tolerance, made mutual indifference a standard of good human relations.

The most that can be said on the side of Locke and Mill, I believe, is that they anticipated this criticism. Both went out of their way to state that they meant to bar only forceful interference by one person in the conduct of another, not admonition, censure, and other such non-violent forms of intervention. But, if a certain sphere of an individual's conduct really does concern himself alone, why is it any more legitimate to enter that sphere through admonition or censure than through force? In admitting a right of peaceful interference, Locke and Mill were trying to stop short of an outright attack on altruism. But this tactic contradicted the whole idea that some things are one person's business and no one else's. Mill was groping toward distinctions very different from the one on which he based his essay—distinctions, for example, between matters in which society can usefully interfere and those that must, like charity or political activity, be left to the discretion of the individual, even though in fact they may not be at all "self-regarding," or distinctions among types of interference, such as force and peaceful admonition. Mill never fully worked out such distinctions, however, and he explicitly based his argument on what might be called (harking back to the honeycomb metaphor) his cellular conception of society.

Let us now turn to traditional arguments of a somewhat different kind. While views of the relationship of individual and society like those we have just been considering probably permeated the whole liberal case for tolerance, the arguments that follow are focused on other realities; they are concerned less with human relations than with belief and truth. Both sets of arguments defend tolerance as necessary for realizing certain relationships between the person and being. The arguments just discussed dealt with these relationships so far as being takes the form of self and others. The arguments to be discussed in the following section deal with them so far as being is an object of cognition.

THE TRADITIONAL ARGUMENTS: BELIEF AND TRUTH

1

"It is absurd," Locke wrote, "that things should be enjoined by laws which are not in men's power to perform. And to believe this or that to be true, does not depend upon our will." [11] This statement contains one of the most appealingly simple of all defenses of tolerance: that belief cannot possibly be determined by force. One can be compelled to act in a certain way but not to think in a certain way. It follows that intolerance is not necessarily evil but altogether futile.

This is one instance in which the two writers we are examining did not share the same position. Mill did not explicitly consider Locke's argument and implicitly contradicted it. He asserted that it is "a piece of idle sentimentality" to suppose that the truth cannot be crushed by force, and he cited historical examples supporting his point. Mill's position was the same as Locke's, in my judgment, only to this extent: he clearly thought that a *reasoned* and *deeply felt* belief could not be determined by force.

That there is some kind of primal incompatibility between force and truth seems to me one of the strongest arguments in favor of tolerance. Later in this essay, I shall suggest a way of formulating this idea that removes the weaknesses in the liberal doctrine. What must be done here, however, is to consider and test the traditional theories, an undertaking that will reveal again, I think, serious inadequacies in the defenses constructed by liberal common sense.

Even Mill's highly qualified position is far from invulnerable. It seems to me that the example of medieval scholasticism casts doubt on the idea that reasoned and deeply felt belief cannot be determined by force. No doubt the medieval scholastics reasoned carefully and even elaborately; some of them presumably believed deeply in the Christian doctrines they were defending—yet at the same time those doctrines were upheld by force. Perhaps it would be unwise to insist very strongly on this argument, for a follower of Mill's might respond that scholastic reasoning always was directed toward predetermined conclusions and thus was not genuine reasoning. He might also question whether Christian beliefs were felt by medieval man as deeply as they would have been had they been altogether freely held. It is doubtful that the issues thus presented can be definitively settled. I do wish to suggest, however, that, even though Mill comes near to an important truth, his explicit argument is far from satisfactory.

A much stronger criticism has to be made of Locke's assertion that "to believe this or that to be true, does not depend on our will." It is, of course, perfectly true that, if I order you to hold a belief you have rejected, you cannot obey me even if you wish to, even if I am a dictator who will torture and kill you if you do not (this is perhaps an unwarranted concession to Locke, for it assumes that effective brainwashing is not possible). But let us complicate the hypothetical situation slightly by supposing that in addition to me, who holds one belief, and you, who holds another, there is a third person who is undecided. By silencing you, I am unlikely to change your mind; but probably I thus reduce your influence over the undecided person and thus increase my own influence over him. It is evident that Locke thought in terms of the two-person hypothesis, but it is the three-person hypothesis that corresponds much more closely with reality. In addition to those with beliefs they can back with force, and those with differing beliefs, there must always be many who are undecided or might become undecided if exposed to conflicting ideas. Hence a regime of force can have a decisive influence on the beliefs that prevail in the society under it. Even a Christian may acknowledge that force had a part in the prevalence of Christianity during the Middle Ages; and today it is presumably not accidental that there are more Communists in Russia than in the United States. The case for tolerance involved an abstraction from historical actuality that made it possible for the versatility of force to be forgotten.

Reflection on the question of what determines belief may serve to introduce us to what is probably the most powerful and complex of all the traditional arguments for tolerance: that tolerance provides an avenue to the truth. The argument will require rather extended explanation and analysis.

2

"The truth certainly would do well enough," Locke wrote, "if she were once left to shift for herself. . . . She is not taught by laws, nor has she any need of force to procure her entrance into the minds of men." [12] If one interprets this statement narrowly, Locke has committed himself to little more than the proposition that tolerance will do no harm. But his words hint at human faculties that assuredly will disclose the truth if given free play. Mill points in the same direction in his famous statement that "the beliefs which we have most warrant for have no safeguard to rest on, but a standing invitation to the whole world to prove them unfounded." [13] In plain terms, the source of truth is the freedom of men to say what they please.

This must be one of the most appealing ideas in the intellectual arsenal of liberal societies. Its origins can be traced back to Socrates and the Athenian agora; and it has inherited some of the eclat of the Renaissance and the Enlightenment as well. Over fifty years after the publication of Mill's essay, Oliver Wendell Holmes expressed his faith in liberated reason (although with little philosophical precision) in a frequently quoted dissenting opinion. "When men have realized that time has upset many fighting faiths," Holmes wrote, "they may come to believe even more than they believe the very foundations of their own conduct that the ultimate good desired is better reached by free trade in ideas—that the best test of truth is the power of the thought to get itself accepted in the competition of the market." [14] One can feel in the breezy toughness of this statement the deep attraction for modern man of the notion that truth is gained though freedom.

It is important to notice, however, that in speaking of truth we are speaking not only of words and propositions but also of the way in which they are apprehended. One does not reach the truth merely by assenting to propositions that are true. Most of us, for example, will accept any proposition concerning physical nature that is set forth, without dissent, by natural scientists, and there are no doubt good reasons for our doing so; but it cannot be said that we thus express our apprehension of the truth. Reaching the truth depends on subjective, as well as objective, factors.

Mill was greatly concerned with this matter, and today, when most of the incontrovertible truth acknowledged by mankind— this being principally scientific knowledge—is fully understood

only by a small number of specialists and means little to the aver-
age individual, who apparently lives in a state of apathetic creduli-
ty, we can perceive that the problem of man's relationship to the
truth is real. For Mill, the solution to the problem lay in tolerance.
An "intelligent and living apprehension" of the truth requires the
same condition as does discovery of the truth, namely, that one
be confronted with ideas contrary to his own and thus be compelled to reason. [15] In this way one discovers not only *what* he
should think, but *why*; it is knowing the reasons supporting an
idea that enables one authentically to apprehend it. If one is ignorant of the supporting reasons, then he is, properly speaking,
ignorant of the truth even when his opinions as a matter of fact
are true. A truth that one accepts but cannot rationally uphold is
"but one superstition the more, accidentally clinging to the words
which enunciate the truth." [16]

Thus there is a strong rationalistic note in Mill's view of the way
truth is apprehended as well as in his view of the way it is discovered. Mill's outlook would be distorted, however, if no notice
were taken of his belief that feeling as well as reason enters into
the matter. Truth is not really apprehended unless it is apprehended
with passion. This does not imply a right to believe something
merely because one very much desires to do so. On the contrary,
the kind of passion Mill called for was a by-product of reason. Reasoning was important to Mill not only because it was the most
promising path to the truth, or because it would enable one fully
to understand an idea; it was important because he thought it was
a source of feeling—of a "living" understanding of things. Thus,
while reason was imperative for Mill, he regarded with aversion the
cold detachment sometimes associated with it.

On the subjective factors involved in reaching the truth, I have
spoken of Mill's views rather than Locke's. This is simply because
Mill discussed the point more fully and forcefully than did Locke.
However, I do not believe that my concentration on Mill involves
any unfairness either to Locke or to the traditional position. Mill's
arguments are for the most part foreshadowed, if not explicitly
stated, in Locke, and they do not seem to me discordant with
either the letter or the spirit of Locke's thinking.

In sum, in a very general form, the traditional argument holds
that tolerance prepares the way for truth both as an outward and

as an inward reality. But in stating this argument I have used some extremely vague phrases—for example, that tolerance "prepares the way" for truth. And little has been said to indicate the concepts of man and truth underlying such a position. Hence the outlines of Locke's and Mill's argument must be sharpened and filled out before any criticisms are offered.

To begin with, exactly how extensive a claim were Locke and Mill making for tolerance? Here we must try to understand their meaning more exactly than they themselves phrased it. Did they mean to assert that tolerance *necessarily* leads to truth? That would be an extreme claim, and since there is nothing in their essays to prove that they meant to make it I think we must assume that they did not. Did they mean to say merely that tolerance is a necessary *condition* for reaching the truth, although it may be only one among a number of such conditions, all equally indispensable? The whole tone of Locke's and Mill's discussion—especially Mill's—is too hopeful to sustain such an interpretation. Hence I think we must conclude that their meaning fell in between the maximal and minimal claims, and that they believed that tolerance was *likely* to lead to the truth.

What views of man and truth underlay this belief? This is an important question, for the main weaknesses of the traditional argument concerning man's relationship to the truth seem to me of a different order than those affecting the argument concerning the relationship of man and man. The latter argument seemed to rest on mistaken goals—individual uniqueness and separateness. The present argument, however, aims at a far less assailable value, that of truth. What is more, the derivation of tolerance from this value, by way of the concept of reason, seems sound. In some sense, the chain of ideas, truth-reasoning-tolerance, is probably valid. The trouble with the traditional argument is that it fails to show *how* it can be valid. It forges a chain that seems necessary for anchoring the idea of tolerance; but while that chain looks strong to common sense, in fact it is weak. Before testing it, let us examine it.

One link in the chain is the idea of human reasonableness. Locke and Mill, and most liberals along with them, have seen tolerance as likely to lead to truth because they have thought that with the opportunities provided by tolerance most people would be likely to engage in reasoning and in this way progress toward the truth; people would reason and would do so successfully. Thus Mill asserted that "there is on the whole a preponderance among mankind of rational opinions and rational conduct." [17]   Locke apparently believed that man's reasonableness could become manifest even in the sphere of religion.

Another link in the chain was that reality is rational; that is, in principle it is subject to complete explanation through a single system of verbal formulas. There is no incongruity between man's reasonableness and the character of reality. By reasoning, man can move toward a full understanding of all things. Mill's commitment to such a view, although accompanied with reservations, is made quite clear in the *System of Logic* (a comprehensive treatise on scientific method, especially as applied in the study of society), as well as being indicated by several comments in the essay *On Liberty*. As for Locke, it is noteworthy that he believed not only in the rationality of physical nature but also, to use the title of one of his lesser works, in "the reasonableness of Christianity."

These assumptions are neither startling nor controversial. Indeed, they are not far from common sense. I should like to suggest, however, that they do not make for a strong case in behalf of tolerance.

The first question we must discuss is whether man is rational enough for the traditional argument to be valid. It must be admitted that man behaves rationally within certain groups—where membership is restricted to people with special intellectual qualifications, where the scope of inquiry is limited by fields of specialization or by the types of questions considered, where proceedings are governed by professional canons of inquiry, and above all, where the participants have no personal material stake in the conclusions reached. A university faculty may be such a group, and a collegial body of judges, like the Supreme Court of the United States, is another. Bodies of this kind do reach objective truth and they may gradually perfect and widen that truth. For them to do this, complete freedom of inquiry is clearly desirable, although perhaps not indispensable (for example, German universities of Kant's time were intellectually vital but not free of censorial supervision).

The idea of tolerance, however, is presumably intended to apply to society as a whole, not merely to small, professionalized groups; it is supposed to apply not only to the specialized research of scholars but also to the search for truths that are philosophical and political in nature; and it was certainly seen by its defenders as applying to matters in which people were intensely—even fanatically—

interested. The question, therefore, is whether man is rational enough to justify the principle that tolerance is likely to be productive of truth when everyone can join in the debate and when every kind of truth is at stake.

Of course, there is no demonstrable answer to this question. Students of human nature—philosophers, psychologists, historians— disagree. But at least it is highly doubtful that men are as rational as Locke and Mill supposed. Several considerations can be cited to support this assertion; all cast shadows over the traditional idea of tolerance.

The first objection is drawn from a very common personal experience, namely, that it is shaking to have one's opinions challenged but reassuring to find that others accept them. Some people, of course, "love to argue," but they are often people for whom argument is a mere game and who never hazard their deepest convictions in the contest. Most of us enjoy discussing questions on which we either have no opinions or have opinions we are willing casually to alter. But few people, if any, can enter equably into a discussion in which their most cherished beliefs are likely to be thrown into doubt. Therefore, when one finds himself in such a discussion he is likely to conduct himself angrily and dogmatically, not rationally. As a result of such an experience, he may feel compelled to re-examine rationally the beliefs thus challenged. That this is exceptional, however, is indicated by a fact well known to students and intellectuals: that an argument almost never changes anyone's mind. The image of man evoked by Mill's arguments for tolerance is that of a being who is composed (although deeply concerned) in the midst of doubt, who is always prepared to change his mind, and who normally emerges from disputes with a more closely reasoned grasp of reality. This is probably an accurate picture of a few people, like Mill himself, as they are most of the time, and of most people as they are now and then. But the experience of each reader will probably support my contention that when ideas clash—and not merely in panel and classroom discussions, where detachment from immediate practical necessities gives reason an exceptional chance to gain ascendancy—Mill's picture of man does not turn out to be an accurate representation of general human behavior.

A glance at history tends to support the same basic conclusion. The ebb and flow of belief, marked often by well-known titles like

"Reformation" or "Enlightenment," strongly suggests the presence of forces far more mysterious than any taken into account by Mill's argument. How much influence did the clash of ideas have in producing the convictions of Sophocles, or of Saint Paul? Some perhaps; and it may have had more in the case of figures like Plato and Saint Augustine. Nevertheless, the greatest spiritual leaders, and the consequences of their lives, point to sources of belief (none the less real for being difficult to specify) that are unrecognized in Mill's essay. These comments may seem lacking in weight since they do not even suggest what does determine the rise and decline of belief; but this question is probably unanswerable, for answering it would require a science of history, and my comments are intended only to express an impression that I think almost every reader of history must gain: that it is given to mankind in some periods of history to discern truth and to feel strong conviction, and in others to be overcome by confusion and apathy, and that institutions such as tolerance do not exercise a determining influence in the matter.

Along with personal experience and history, does not the economic environment of every twentieth-century American testify to the limits of human rationality? It is not an exaggeration (and it is far short of Marxist claims) to say that the main uses to which freedom of expression has been put are commercial and financial. Of course, not all speech is directly concerned with buying and selling. But a great deal of it is; this is evident in the prominence of advertisements in magazines and newspapers and of commercials on television. In addition, there is a serious question as to whether those communications not overtly commercial are truly independent of commercial interests and relationships. No doubt, the kind of tolerance prevailing in America does occasionally allow truth to break forth and to unsettle established powers and interests in a way that could not happen under a dictatorial and intolerant system. But one need not be an orthodox Marxist to feel that Americans, with all of their freedom, show far greater concern for material goods than for truth. This presumably would not be the case if the psychology presupposed by the liberal defenders of tolerance were valid.

Herbert Marcuse and others have argued that the ostensible tolerance of Americans is altogether fraudulent, that in fact it is a "repressive tolerance." [18]   According to these writers, a variety of conditions assures that critics of the established order will not be fairly heard. The conclusion either hinted at or explicitly drawn is that those victimized by this deceptively stifling arrangement, that is, radicals and other critics of things as they are, need not be bound by the canons of tolerance; they are justified in using violence until society has been reconstructed in a way that will make tolerance genuine. My own view is that this analysis contains exaggerations and that the invitation to intolerance that is drawn from it is too unqualified. The qualifications that should attend any such invitation will be considered later in this essay. It does seem to me, however, that Marcuse and the writers allied with him have, at least in their criticisms, made a substantial point. There is an immense disparity between the formalities and the actualities of freedom in the United States; the range of what can legally be said is almost limitless, whereas the range of what is likely to be seriously listened to is narrow. This disparity would be inexplicable were men as rational as liberals like Locke and Mill have assumed.

The final consideration I shall cite as casting doubt on the premise of human rationality is the simplest but perhaps the most persuasive. That is the scope and intensity of violence in the twentieth century—violence that has exploded not only among nations, as in two world wars, but also within nations, as in Spain in the thirties or Vietnam in the sixties. The violence of our era has sometimes seemed rationally justifiable, as with the American response to Japan's attack on Pearl Harbor, and at other times it has seemed to express a terrifying irrationality, as with the Nazi death camps. Surely, it is only by continuing unthinkingly to hold on to a set of ideas inherited from a more pacific, and seemingly more reasonable, period of history that we are able in our own bloody times to entertain the idea that man is rational.

All of this, it may be said, is very impressionistic. But can an argument on this sort of question be anything else? The reader may feel that reference should be made to the conclusions of experts. It is doubtful that true experts exist in the area we are considering; it is doubtful even that they could exist. However, there have been eminent writers, and there are highly developed schools of thought concerned with the nature of man, and it may be worth checking the present argument against their conclusions.

As noted above, students of human nature are not wholly in agreement. So far as they are, however, they strengthen the argument I am making. I shall cite only three of the best-known contemporary views among people who have seriously studied and reflected upon man. 1.   Psychoanalysis seems to show that man's beliefs are determined far less by reality or by discourse than by the pressure of inner conflict; men generally are preoccupied, largely to the exclusion of objectivity and reflection, with the effort to handle the monstrous demands made on them by repressed desires. 2.   For Marx and most of his followers, the primary determinant of belief is one's economic situation; it is preoccupation with economic necessity that rules out the deliberative life that Mill implicitly attributes to men. 3.   Existentialists typically find the origins of belief in an irrational act of choice through which one establishes a certain relationship between himself and reality; thus Kierkegaard, the originator of existentialism, urged man to seek a summit of faith that could be gained only by a "leap"—a decision uncalled for, or even forbidden, by reason.

I do not mean to impose simple meanings on complex currents of thought. Disagreements are profound not only among these schools but also within them; their authority is weakened by these divisions. Further, none of them denies for all persons and all occasions the possibility of a deliberative approach to reality. They do, however, present an image of man sharply at variance with the one underlying the traditional argument for tolerance.

These four points, with the supporting testimony cited above, tend to show that man is less rational than Locke and Mill supposed. They do not show that man is altogether irrational but only that he is not the deliberative being that the traditional argument for tolerance seems to assume. Let us suppose that this conclusion is valid. What is its effect on the ideal of tolerance?

Certainly, the ideal itself is not overturned, for the possibility remains that it can be defended on other grounds. Nor is the idea that tolerance is justified in connection with the search for truth overturned; it may make a contribution of a kind that Locke and Mill did not consider. But it seems to me that the case made by Locke and Mill, the classical case for tolerance, is seriously shaken. One cannot continue to think of tolerance as justified on the grounds that under its protection men are likely to begin reasoning and through their reasoning they are likely to reach the truth. Neither Locke nor Mill builds effective defenses against the suspicion that tolerance may eventuate in doubt and confusion and that truth may be discovered under conditions of restricted freedom.

It may be urged in Mill's behalf that, far from having unlimited confidence in the rationality of the general populace, he feared democracy and the reign of public opinion. This must be granted; it is made quite evident in the essay *On Liberty*. But he never fully defined, or drew out the political implications of, this fear. Had he done so, he would have been compelled to qualify severely his support for tolerance.

What we have been discussing so far is *psychological* rationalism—the view that man is rational. This must be distinguished from *ontological* rationalism, according to which reality is accessible to reason. As I brought out above, the latter as well as the former seems to be presupposed in the traditional argument for tolerance. In fact, it is possible to argue—as I shall in the following chapter—that reality is not rational but that reason still has a role in searching for the truth. But such a view is strange by the standards of the traditional liberal outlook and did not enter into Locke's or Mill's argument, at least not consciously. They held that reality is rational in the sense that reason can penetrate and surround it, as it were, thus leading to comprehensive scientific understanding. Having discussed the psychological rationalism underlying the classical idea of tolerance, it seems appropriate now to consider the ontological rationalism on which it also rested.

The subject is a very large one and will be more fully discussed in the following chapter. But in our explorations here of the fallacies in the traditional doctrine of tolerance I hope it will suffice to point to the radical difference, apparently inherent in the nature of human faculties, between the conclusions of reason and the disclosures of immediate experience. The former are abstract, the latter, concrete; the former are general, the latter, particular. Reason strives to bring all reality within closed systems, while experience is endless and cannot be wholly comprised in a set of rational formulas. Reason objectifies reality, but even the experience of reasoning itself includes a reality, the one who reasons—the subject—that cannot be viewed as an object, as a desk or a book can be. Reason summarizes the past, whereas immediate experience contains awareness of an undecided future.

What must be particularly noted in connection with this divergence is that reason is unable to reconcile the two sides in its own favor. It is, so to speak, a party to the dispute and thus it cannot also adjudicate it. Less metaphorically, reason cannot show that the disclosures of immediate experience are secondary in any sense to its own disclosures; it cannot show that reality is of the nature of the logically interrelated universals that are the objects of reason. One seems justified in concluding, therefore, that the concept of reality as wholly accessible to reason accords neither with immediate experience nor with the verdicts of reason.

These observations may seem very inconclusive. As noted, the task of working out the main idea contained in them will be undertaken in the following chapter. Some weight may be added to them, however, by noting that they express fragmentarily and crudely a conviction powerful in twentieth-century thinking: that, since we have no grounds for setting aside as delusory the disclosures of immediate experience, being must be envisioned as concrete, nonobjective, and undecided. This conviction is most strikingly manifest in existentialism and phenomenology, but it is influential far beyond the bounds of these particular schools. [19]

Looking at things from this hypothetical vantage point, one would have to say that even if human beings were rational they would not be able rationally to comprehend reality. Thus the traditional doctrine of tolerance is called into question from another angle. Since that doctrine is premised on both psychological and ontological rationalism, showing the latter to be questionable imperils it no less than attacking the former. The assumption that reality is not rational does not bar every connection between reason and tolerance, since reason might possibly play a part in a process it is inherently incapable of bringing to consummation. But it does bar the kind of connection that Mill apparently conceived of and that Locke apparently had in mind: one in which reason leads directly to a rational grasp of reality.

To base tolerance on the twofold premise that human beings are rational and reality is accessible to reason is questionable not only because of the dubiousness of the premise, however; even granting the premise, the argument deriving from it runs into trouble. In order to see this, let us assume for the moment that most people are reasonable and that reality can be wholly comprehended in a single system of propositions. The argument that tolerance is required by our concern for truth is still exposed to at least two serious objections.

The less compelling of these is that if human beings have the capacity for rationally understanding reality in its entirety—if human powers are so great as this—it would seem that reason might be able not only to survive under a measure of authoritarian control but even to prosper were such control properly organized. Mill eloquently denounced the sentimental notion that truth is impervious to repression. One may agree with him here, and in addition study sympathetically all of his arguments in behalf of tolerance, and still retain the suspicion that, given Mill's conceptions of man and reason, the search for truth might be successfully carried forward under some kind of dictatorial management. It may be that truth can readily be crushed, and that complete freedom of expression is advantageous in the search for truth; yet it still is possible that absolute authority may in some ways facilitate the search for objective truth. The progress of Soviet science, even with the setbacks marked by the Lysenko affair, seems to indicate that this may be the case.

The more serious objection that arises when one has accepted the premises of the traditional argument is this: if we must be tolerant in order to learn the truth, and tolerance successfully leads us to that end, it must then render itself superfluous. In other words, to regard tolerance as a means to the truth is, assuming the rationality of man and of reality, to regard it as a temporary expedient. Mill was fully conscious of this difficulty. In one of the most interesting passages in his essay, he asserts that "the number of doctrines which are no longer disputed or doubted will be constantly on the increase." Then he acknowledges that this development, although clearly progressive, will render tolerance increasingly gratuitous so far as it is necessary for the discovery of truth. Truth will be less and less in doubt. Mill's response is to suggest that the intellectual conflict necessitating tolerance be artificially kept alive. He expresses the hope that "the teachers of mankind" will, in the course of communicating knowledge, try to devise "some contrivance for making the difficulties of the question as present to the learner's consciousness, as if they were pressed upon him by a dissentient champion, eager for his conversion." [20] In other words, Mill falls back on the argument that tolerance is necessary, if not for establishing truth, for gaining a vital relationship with it.

In these passages, Mill sets an example of ingenious and candid argumentation. But I think that his case suffers more serious damage than is apparent at a glance. For he has, in effect, conceded that, so far as we are rational and are interrelated through knowledge, tolerance is not a standard of human relations. In other words, the ideal human state indicated by Mill, and I think implicit in the rationalism of many liberals, is non-tolerant (it cannot be termed "intolerant" because, by hypothesis, all know the truth and hence there are no divergent opinions of which to be either tolerant or intolerant). As for Mill's hope that free discussion will survive through doubts deliberately contrived, and then deliberately removed, surely artificial disputation of this kind does not call for anything that can properly be termed "tolerance." To be tolerant is to be self-restrained in an encounter with something which, at least at the outset, is strange and disturbing. Dealing with a doubt one has deliberately implanted is not an encounter of this kind and does not require tolerance.

This criticism of the traditional position would be taken too lightly if it were assumed to apply only to a utopia of scientific certainty lying in the distant future. Those of Mill's persuasion must believe that truth is steadily becoming more perfect and comprehensive. This implies, however, that the area in which tolerance is needed is steadily shrinking. One who looked upon his own age as progressive and enlightened would necessarily view tolerance not merely as a temporary expedient but also as having only a restricted application. The philosophical authoritarianism of Plato exhibits the political possibilities inherent in the faith in reason no less clearly than does the liberalism of Mill.

These criticisms lead in no single direction. Not only might each criticism be developed divergently from the others; but diverse conclusions might be drawn even from a single criticism. For example, the significance of the first criticism—that human beings are not altogether rational—depends on how one answers a number of questions that arise out of it: do we have some faculty other than reason—for example, intuition—through which we can apprehend reality and govern our conduct? To what extent are human beings equal in moral and political insight? Are there any moral rules or values that would dictate tolerance for its own sake and regardless of consequences? Depending on how these questions are answered, the critique of psychological rationalism might be developed into a doctrine of charismatic leadership or of instinctive popular wisdom. Or tolerance might be considered necessary for making us aware of our rational uncertainty, this being the alternative that will be argued in the following chapter. The critique of ontological rationalism could be developed along parallel lines.

Thus no particular doctrine counter to Mill's can be read into these criticisms. It cannot even be concluded that Mill's general position, assuming the validity of these criticisms, is totally untenable; there are many different ways, as the above paragraph suggests, of holding and defending a position. But I do think the conclusion can be drawn that the traditional liberal view of tolerance as the way to truth is highly dubious.

Let us briefly examine one more argument turning on the nature of belief. Strictly construed, it is implicit in the arguments already discussed and hence stands or falls with those; but it is encountered so frequently, and it brings out so clearly a difficult and important set of issues involved in the ideal of tolerance, that it deserves separate consideration.

3

One should be tolerant of the ideas of others, so this argument usually runs, because one's own ideas may be in error. Locke, without thrusting such a statement right in front of readers who, in his age, were often sure that their ideas were *not* in error, makes clear his adherence to the attitude it expresses. "The controversy between these churches about the truth of their doctrines, and the purity of their worship," he wrote, "is on both sides equal; nor is there any judge, either at Constantinople or elsewhere upon earth, by whose sentence it can be determined." [21]   Mill is even more definite, and he relies very heavily, in his defense of tolerance, on the proposition that "we can never be sure that the opinion we are endeavouring to stifle is a false opinion." [22]   Going somewhat further, and perhaps unnecessarily jeopardizing his argument, he asserts that "all silencing of discussion is an assumption of infallibility." [23]   Oliver Cromwell gives a moving statement of the same idea in his famous injunction to his self-certain countrymen at a time of civil conflict: "I beseech you, in the bowels of Christ, think it possible you may be mistaken."

How can such sane counsel be rejected? Surely, one of the most unchallengeable things that can be said about human beings is that singly and collectively they are liable to err. Socrates, who was regarded as the wisest man of his time, not only by the Delphian oracle but by many succeeding generations, asserted that his only claim to superior wisdom lay in his awareness not simply of his fallibility but of his ignorance. A person who, on any point outside the bounds of exact science or verifiable facts, refused to admit that he might be mistaken would seem arrogant and possibly dangerous.

My own view is that Cromwell's counsel (and Locke's and Mill's) must, in some form, be accepted. But not only is it far more difficult to do so than is generally recognized; it is difficult even to understand that counsel—to comprehend the nature and possibility of the attitude called for. Accordingly, the criticism to which the traditional argument is subject is not that it reaches a false conclusion but that difficulties in the way of that conclusion are not taken into account and that the conclusion is even less comprehensible than it seems.

In centering on this one criticism, I will be paying little attention to two others that are relevant to the traditional argument— criticisms which are not so negligible as to be passed over without mention but which, for various reasons, do not demand development in an essay designed to be brief and comprehensive. The less important of these is that Mill seems to confuse being absolutely sure on one particular point with a general claim to infallibility. But it is possible for me to say that on one particular matter I cannot be mistaken—this might be a fact I personally observed, or it might be a matter of religious faith—without implying that I am infallible. I do not dwell on this criticism because it seems to me that while Mill's argument may draw some unwarranted rhetorical force from the confusion, since it seems particularly monstrous that someone should claim to be not merely right but infallible, the substance of his argument is not seriously affected by it; convinced of the confusion, he could have removed it without materially altering his position.

The second of these minor criticisms is somewhat more serious: tolerance does not follow with absolute logical necessity from an acknowledgement of possible error. When I have admitted, "I may be mistaken," I am bound to conclude, "I must not silence free discussion," only if I have made several intervening assumptions, none of which I am compelled to make. I must assume that, although I may not know the truth, the truth still can be known; otherwise any kind of inquiry would be useless. I must assume also that free discussion is necessary for reaching the truth; if it is not, then I may silence my opponents but reach the truth through inspiration, intuition, or some other means. Finally, I must assume that the truth is worth reaching; if enjoying power, through such acts as making others think what I think, is a higher value than knowing the truth, then I am not obliged to allow free discussion, even though that would lead to the truth. In short, contrary to the supposition of Locke and Mill, as well as that of other tolerant people, there is nothing self-contradictory about admitting that one's own opinions may be erroneous while silencing all counter-opinions.

None of the requisite assumptions is self-evident. Nevertheless, it seems legitimate to grant them here. The second, having to do with the relationship of tolerance and truth, has already been discussed. The first and third, to the effect that truth can be known and is worth knowing, not only accord with the common sense of most people but, I think, are genuinely valid (although not self-evident). Thus to question them here probably would not lead into fruitful areas of investigation.

Let us, then, turn to the major point: that to recognize genuinely that one may be mistaken puts one in a far more uncomfortable and paradoxical position than is recognized in the traditional defense of tolerance. It is, of course, easy to say, "I believe such and such, but I may be mistaken." Indeed, because it is considered to be good form, we often do so in the course of discussions. I suggest, however, that we allow ourselves to suppose that, because it is easy to *say* it, it is easy to *think* it. But it is reasonable to ask whether actually thinking it is even possible, let alone easy. It appears that believing something is believing that I am *not* mistaken; on the other hand, so far as I come to feel that I may be mistaken in holding to some idea or doctrine, I cease believing it. I may, of course, combine a degree of belief with a degree of doubt. But, if my belief is assured, then the degree of doubt must be so small as to make it questionable whether discussion is worth the trouble. On the other hand, so far as discussion assumes greater importance under the pressure of increasing doubt, my assurance must decline. Most liberal defenders of tolerance speak as though it is easy simultaneously to believe and to doubt. But, according to the common meaning of words, to believe is to overcome doubt and to doubt is to suspend belief. Thus what liberals often think of as matter-of-course decency appears in actuality to be self-contradictory.

Can the tension perhaps be resolved by giving up everything on the side of belief and accepting pure doubt? Can we say simply that a tolerant person must be a skeptic? One who is tolerant, not because he simultaneously believes and doubts, as required by the traditional argument, but because he believes nothing and simply doubts, is not burdened with the tension of a divided mind.

Locke and Mill, however, would have rejected any such escape from the dilemma. Locke, although tentative and open-minded in his intellectual procedures, was far from a skeptic; in philosophy he espoused a number of ontological and ethical doctrines and in religion he was firmly committed to Christianity. As for Mill, his expectation that science would provide conclusive knowledge not only of the physical universe but of man and society as well has already been discussed. Both figures, in not only having convictions but in believing that people should have convictions, seem to typify the liberal attitude. Liberalism has often involved beliefs that are commonplace or pallid, but it has not normally involved extreme skepticism.

In any case, skepticism provides no real escape from the dilemma. If a person does not believe anything, then he does not believe any of the assumptions set forth above as being necessary in order to infer from the proposition "I may be mistaken" the conclusion "I must not silence discussion." He does not in that case believe that truth can be known, that free discussion leads to the truth, or that truth is worth reaching. More simply, if he does not believe in anything, he does not believe in tolerance. Doubt is wholly destructive of tolerance, unless it is in some way combined with belief.

Then perhaps the tension can be relieved by disposing of doubt and believing with no reservations. The most obvious objection to such a proposal is that a state of untroubled belief is at present, and perhaps forever, beyond our reach. Doubt cannot be defeated merely by an act of will. But, even if it could, it is unlikely that this would strengthen tolerance. Let us imagine a man who has no doubts about anything. If the proposition that every person should be allowed to say what he pleases is among the things he does not doubt, then he would be tolerant. But he probably would not accept such a proposition, for if he respected the truth and other men, he would inevitably be inclined to force upon others the truth that he does not doubt. Further, even if, owing to some intervening assumption such as the impossibility of forcing a person to believe, he were tolerant in his certitude, his tolerance would inevitably be mixed with indifference, condescension, or contempt.

Thus tolerance must apparently be based on a mixture of belief and doubt. It follows that the traditional argument is formally correct. What is lacking in that argument is recognition of the paradoxical nature of the attitude it demands and thus explanation of its possibility. Locke and Mill accurately indicate one of the ground principles of tolerance but fail to elucidate that principle, to provide convincing reasons why one should accept it, or even to show that the principle is not self-contradictory.

Only one remaining argument in favor of tolerance needs to be considered. This argument concerns the historical effects of tolerance. The term "historical effects" is intended here to refer to effects on the social world around us in contradistinction to the "inner" effects discussed in the present section.

THE TRADITIONAL ARGUMENTS:
TOLERANCE AND HISTORY

Locke claims less for tolerance, in terms of historical effects, than does Mill, although, in a discouraged age like today, what he claims looks like quite a bit. Tolerance, he asserts or implies in several passages, leads to order and peace. Locke wanted to rebut the notion, common in his day, that tolerance encouraged disorder by permitting religious factions. "There is only one thing which gathers people into seditious commotions," he asserted, "and that is oppression." [24] Thus "seditious commotions" can be expected to die out when oppression is replaced by tolerance. Of course, the scope of Locke's argument was restricted. He said only that *religious* disorders and wars are provoked by *religious* intolerance. However, if his argument is extended beyond the domain of religion, it suggests that order and peace are spontaneous and thus will tend to prevail wherever there is freedom. A Lockean today would presumably argue that political extremists of right and left will be dangerous only if we try to suppress them. He would recommend tolerance on the grounds that it would encourage everyone to be orderly and peaceful.

Mill thought that tolerance would lead to a greater good than mere order—that is, progress. "The only unfailing and permanent source of improvement is liberty," he wrote, "since by it there are as many possible independent centres of improvement as there are individuals." [25]   It is worth noting how unqualified a statement this is: liberty is not merely favorable to progress or merely a pre-requisite to progress. It is an "unfailing and permanent source" of progress.

The difference between Locke and Mill does not seem worth dwelling upon. Locke lived near the end of a period, initiated pri-marily by the fragmentation and fanaticism of the Reformation, during which the overriding political problem was order. Although Locke was concerned with problems other than order, such as con-stitutionalism and the rights of property, the preoccupations of his time drew his attention to the question of order when he con-sidered the historical effects of toleration. In Mill's time, however, almost two centuries later, order was no longer so overwhelming a problem as it had been, and, in response to the feelings of a civil-ization grown more worldly and self-confident, the idea of progress had become popular. Thus Mill expressed his belief in tolerance by connecting it with progress. What Locke and Mill have in common is confidence that tolerance is historically beneficial. They envi-sioned the benefits to be expected differently, since they lived in different times. The attitudes of both toward the historical conse-quences of tolerance, however, can be described with no exaggera-tion as complacent. Tolerance was almost certain to be salutary.

Underlying this conclusion was a premise likewise shared by the two thinkers: that man's nature is such that when freed he is apt to perform acts that are historically beneficial. He is spontaneously orderly and spontaneously progressive.

The validity of the conclusion depends largely on that of the premise. If Locke's and Mill's appraisal of human nature is accurate, their assessment of the probable historical effects of tolerance must be accepted; if they viewed man too uncritically, however, their historical expectations must be regarded as baseless. But their hope was based not only on an optimistic appraisal of human nature but on another factor as well. This was a belief in what is often referred to as "the natural harmony of interests." The idea that even selfish-ness was not necessarily a source of disharmony derived partly, in Locke's case, from an assumption that there is so much open land in the world that human interests need not seriously clash, and partly from a tendency (of which Locke was perhaps not fully conscious and which Mill was trying, but not very effectually, to overcome) to trust the natural economic laws set in motion by a free market to counterbalance the evil effects of selfishness. The result was that the two thinkers could be hopeful about the future without being utterly blind to man's weaknesses. I think we are justified in passing by this attitude and allowing the issue to be decided in terms of human nature, for two reasons. The first is that the idea of a natural harmony of interests has been so largely discredited that it hardly seems to need refuting; it is still possible to think that an unregulated market is the best way of organizing certain delimited areas of activity, but not to think, in the style of nineteenth-century laissez faire, that natural laws can be relied upon to transform the results of altogether materialistic and self-seeking behavior into public order and progress. The second reason for setting aside the idea of natural harmony is that it is primarily economic and thus only tangentially related to the question of tolerance. It inspires a mood that pervades the thought of Locke and Mill but is not a concept that can give much support to their views on intellectual freedom.

Does everything, then, rest on the question, already discussed, as to whether man is rational? Obviously, something depends on this; Locke and Mill were historically optimistic in part from believing that reality could be known through reason and that men on the whole were reasonable. Thus, in some measure a judgment concerning the historical effects of tolerance was implicit in the conclusions reached in the preceding section. If it has been shown that Locke and Mill relied too heavily on reason, then their historical optimism has been placed in doubt. The whole question, however, is broader than the one we have considered. The historical hopefulness of the traditional argument depends on assuming that man is not only able with his reason to inquire successfully into reality but is also disposed to be guided by the results. The assumption that man *lives* rationally goes beyond the assumption that he *thinks* rationally, and confidence that tolerance will eventuate in order and progress depends on the wider assumption.

The question before us, then, is whether on the whole man is constructive and co-operative; only if he is can tolerance be justified on the grounds that it is productive of order and progress. I suggest that the first step in answering the question consists in recognizing that no apodictic answer is possible. I suggest also, however, that in this condition itself—the unknowability of man—there ironically lies a partial answer.

If man could finally be understood as thoroughly as a machine, then it might be possible to specify exactly the extent to which he can be trusted. As I have already pointed out, however, man is not only the object known but also the knowing subject. The idea that man might be wholly known involves a tacit denial of the subject-object structure that encompasses and limits all knowledge. Moreover, man, as each one encounters him in the form of the self, is apparently free, and this gives rise to the question as to how his behavior ever can be predicted. Foreseeing what we are going to do, we are able to do something else. A social scientist might reply that *some* will be able to foresee what *others* will do. But, in this case, are not those who do the foreseeing the unpredictable, and thus unknowable, factor? Finally, man is disclosed in moods and emotions that can never be embodied in precise, objective, and transmittable knowledge. For example, no one else knows, or can possibly know, how I feel about my wife and sons, about death, or about the countryside in which I grew to manhood. Occasionally, of course, another person may help me to understand myself—but not by stating a piece of objective knowledge about me that I am compelled to accept; another person can only suggest possibilities of self-understanding that I must test in an area of inner life to which no one else can possibly be admitted.

Here I am dealing summarily, of course, with complex questions. But the point I am suggesting is quite simple, and it has been concisely embodied in words that often recur in the writings of Karl Jaspers: man is always more than he can know about himself. If this is so, then it is impossible to pass final judgment on him.

This very impossibility, however, constitutes a partial answer to the question as to how far man can be trusted. We cannot rest confidence in one whom we cannot know. The unavailability of an affirmative answer constitutes a negative answer. Locke and Mill relied too casually on a being who is inevitably mysterious.

But, although no definite and final judgments concerning man can be made, it is possible to surmise. We can look at man as he has disclosed himself in experience and ask how far liberal confidence in the results to be anticipated from tolerance *appears* to be justified. This will not provide us with conclusive knowledge, but it may enable us to reach an informed guess. There are two basic ways of consulting experience.

One of these is introspective. Each of us, by being human, has access to an inexhaustible source of insights concerning man. To draw on this source, one must, as Thomas Hobbes advised, "read in himself, not this or that particular man; but mankind." [26] What is disclosed in such a reading? I shall suggest an answer and ask the reader to consider, again quoting Hobbes, "if he also find not the same in himself," for, as Hobbes added, "this kind of doctrine admitteth no other demonstration." [27]

I suggest that a reading of oneself discloses—in addition to other qualities—persistent selfishness, persistent pride, and cunning. "Persistent selfishness" designates the tendency, only partially and occasionally overcome, to care far more about one's own welfare than about the welfare of others; "persistent pride" refers to the tenacious desire to gain ascendancy over others—through prestige, knowledge, riches, or some other means; in suggesting that man is "cunning," I am thinking not just of deliberate actions but of the selfishness and pride which often circumvent the most resolute efforts to overcome them, so that a candid and perceptive look at a virtuous act (which usually can be given only introspectively and thus only in connection with a "virtuous act" of one's own) often turns up a selfish or prideful motive. To modern heirs of Locke and Mill, such hypotheses may seem morbid. Are they not, however, broadly in accordance with such great works of introspection as the *Confessions* of Augustine and the novels of Dostoevsky? Does the reader's own self-reading fundamentally contradict them?

The other way of consulting experience is historical; it requires, in contrast with introspection, looking outward and attempting to discern human nature in the events of the past. A reading of historical man discloses as little to justify the trust expressed in the traditional argument as does a reading of oneself. History is a record of war, civil turmoil, sickness, and failure. It is also, of course, a record of cultural and political achievements such as those exemplified by Periclean Athens and the Roman Empire. Such achievements, however, can never be interpreted simply as victories on the part of virtue; the glories of Periclean Athens were dependent on imperialism and slavery, and the peace of the Roman Empire was a product in part of despotism and ruthless warfare. Moreover, such achievements are always temporary, passing either quickly and catastrophically, like the ancient city-state, or slowly (though perhaps still catastrophically), like Rome. Thus Hegel wrote of history that

> when we look at this display of passions, and the consequences of their violence; the Unreason which is associated not only with them, but even (rather we might say *especially*) with *good* designs and righteous aims; when we see the evil, the vice, the ruin that has befallen the most flourishing kingdoms which the mind of man ever created; we can scarce avoid being filled with sorrow at this universal taint of corruption. [28]

During the past two or three hundred years, there has been a disposition to consign the evils of history primarily to the past and to anticipate their complete disappearance in the future; this disposition produced the doctrine of progress. It seems to me, however, that Reinhold Niebuhr is right in asserting that this doctrine has been refuted by events. Our own time, like the times Hegel contemplated, "forms a picture of most fearful aspect." [29]

Thus, to state as moderate a conclusion as possible, Locke and Mill seem rather heedless in their appraisal of man; they take insufficient account of his mysterious nature and unforeseeable ways, and they give too little weight to the selfishness, pride, and cunning found both in oneself and in history. Consequently, the argument for tolerance that they base on the prospect of historical benefits is dubious. If men are not spontaneously orderly or spontaneously progressive, then the results of liberating them must be uncertain. Locke has no warrant for promising, as casually as he does, that toleration will quiet "seditious commotions," and Mill is not justified in characterizing liberty as "the only unfailing and permanent source of improvement."

THE BASIC ASSUMPTIONS

We have considered six traditional arguments in favor of tolerance, two concerned with the relations of individual and society, three with belief and truth, and one with historical consequences. These arguments, however, abstract as they may have seemed, are not the deepest foundations of the traditional doctrine of tolerance. The principles that are the ultimate bedrock of tolerance have often seemed so unchallengeable to liberal thinkers like Locke and Mill that they did not bother even to formulate and defend them. Three such principles can be seen underneath the arguments I have discussed; these correspond roughly, but not precisely, to the three sections in which the arguments were grouped. For the sake of convenience, I shall refer to these three principles as individualism, rationalism, and historical optimism.

Individualism   The traditional arguments presuppose that human beings are, and ought to be, separate from one another. This, of course, is true only relatively; thinkers like Locke and Mill do not perceive or demand a complete separation of man from man. They are strongly inclined, however, to speak as though life at its best is carried on by individuals who are connected with others only peripherally and incidentally. This attitude is pronounced in the first group of arguments: the highest values are autonomy and uniqueness, and each individual can strive for these values without significantly affecting the lives of others. However, the individualistic attitude can be seen also in the argument that belief cannot be determined by force; the plausibility of the argument, as was noted, depends on a drastic oversimplification of social relationships. Further evidence of individualism is Mill's assertion that progress is assured only when all individuals are "independent centres of improvement."

Rationalism   I have alluded to this principle in speaking of the concept of man as a "deliberative creature." It is assumed in the traditional arguments—particularly in those concerned with belief and truth, which make up the second group—that man is markedly rational, both in his capacities and in his inclinations. Thus he cannot be made to believe through force; when he is challenged by beliefs counter to his own, instead of reacting with violence, or recoiling into a state of solitude and doubt, he re-examines the grounds of his position; when convictions collide the result is not confusion but truth; and one can readily admit that he may be mistaken because with a little patience and effort his mistakes can be corrected. Accompanying this view of man, which I have termed "psychological rationalism," and in some ways supporting it, is an "ontological rationalism." Reality is rational, as is the human mind, and thus is subject to total comprehension.

Historical optimism   According to the traditional liberal viewpoint, tolerance is not simply a moral obligation that must be fulfilled regardless of the consequences of doing so. It does not even exact a price for its benefits. It promises definite and unmixed historical gains. The ultimate grounds of this viewpoint lie in the twofold notion that man is reasonable and that reality conforms with his character. It follows that the spontaneous movement of human activity is toward an ever more reasonable life. Tolerance, therefore, is not dangerous or problematic; it is simply good policy. It is a way of liberating the orderly and progressive tendencies in human nature, thus furthering the ascendant course of history.

These three principles, individualism, rationalism, and historical optimism, underlie the traditional ideal of tolerance. Men are basically distinct, thoughtful, and constructive, and reality lends itself to their understanding and control. Hence tolerance is both fair and beneficial. This view pervades both the *Letter Concerning Toleration* and the essay *On Liberty*; and is, I think, widespread among those who have established and supported tolerance in various Western societies during the past few centuries.

The historical power of these principles goes far beyond the issues being considered in this essay. For example, the traditional theory of constitutional democracy is individualistic in its stress on the importance of personal property and personal freedom; it is rationalistic in its reliance on man's capacity to discern, and his disposition to obey, natural law; it is historically optimistic in virtue of the assumption that natural forces in history will inevitably spread and perfect democratic institutions. Another example of the far-reaching influence of the three principles, the economic theory of "free enterprise," held that most constructive economic activities are carried on by single, unregulated individuals; it regarded these individuals as highly rational in the pursuit of profit; and it maintained that the fruits of economic freedom would be prosperity and justice. The truth is that individualism, rationalism, and historical optimism are the main characteristics of the modern middle-class mind—of the mind that has, more than any other, shaped the political and economic order of Western nations during the past few centuries.

My criticisms of the traditional arguments for tolerance are in substance criticisms of these underlying principles. If the criticisms are sound, it follows that the ideal of tolerance must be placed on new foundations, or abandoned. To explore the possibility of new foundations is the aim of the following chapter. But first I think it is in order to note that the author's doubts concerning these principles are not his alone. Individualism, rationalism, and historical optimism are being abandoned by many, and the question of whether tolerance can be grounded anew bears on the question of whether it can retain sufficient allegiance to survive.

THE PASSING OF THE TRADITIONAL ASSUMPTIONS

The current abandonment of liberal principles has probably been expressed more dramatically by the so-called New Left than by any other group. Here the central ideal has been something very unlike individualism—participatory democracy. The traditional idea that democracy can be defined largely in terms of individual rights and that it is enacted primarily in the solitude of the voting booth has been rejected. Democracy has been construed rather as common action and as common enjoyment of the fruits of action. What is more, New Left radicals have probably moved as far away from the rationalism of the liberals as from their individualism. Man is envisioned as primarily moral rather than rational—as capable of know-knowing instinctively what justice requires in every situation without the need to take time for discussion or thought. Thus, for example, in campus disturbances the mood of radical students has been one of passionate righteousness, with counterarguments—glorified by Mill as the only possible source of assurance—suffered impatiently if at all. As for historical optimism, it must be acknowledged that the left has not rejected that view of things so unambiguously as it has individualism and rationalism; radical students have sometimes seemed as certain as were philosophers of the Enlightenment that a new world is in the making. New Left attitudes toward existing society, however, have manifested a sensitivity to the selfishness, pride, and cunning of the dominant groups that contrasts sharply with the tendency of liberals to assume that, while many improvements are needed, men can be relied upon to make them peacefully and co-operatively.

Many people, of course, not only dissent from such views but deeply resent them. Some of the most outspoken opponents of the New Left, however, have also moved away from the individualism, rationalism, and historical optimism of the liberal tradition. I am thinking of those often classified as conservatives. The value they set over all others is not the individual but the nation; the style of life they encourage is one not of critical rationality but of stern dutifulness, in which laws are obeyed and military service rendered without questioning national traditions or governmental policies; they are mistrustful of man and uneasy about the future, as is shown in their preoccupation with law, order, and discipline.

Radicals and conservatives, of course, do not make up the whole of society; large numbers of those in between still hold to the tradition represented by Locke and Mill. Even among liberals, however, there have been widespread defections from individualism, rationalism, and historical optimism with respect to at least one set of problems—those of economics. Liberals now commonly assume that men are so interdependent economically that the solitary individual is helpless and must therefore ally himself with groups such as trade unions and call in the aid of government; liberals today typically assume that the basic rules of justice, and their general meaning in most situations, are clear enough for us to need effective organization more than varying opinions and free discussion; and their trust in man has been so far undermined that, when they think of problems like air pollution and poverty, they regard the future with apprehension rather than with hope.

Perhaps the traditional assumptions will make a comeback; perhaps, at least, they are not as near extinction as my remarks suggest. There are still eloquent, as well as silent but powerful, defenders of individualistic economics; many cultivated and responsible people (the late Walter Lippmann is an eminent example) are emphatically in the camp of rationalism; and even the idea of progress, probably the most beleaguered of the three assumptions, has not been wholly abandoned, as is evidenced in the hopeful rhetoric of American politicians. In the past, however, probably no idea has remained ascendant for more than a few centuries; the reign of liberal ideas has extended over two or three centuries of incomparably swift development, and its time may well be passing. Moreover, it is very difficult for most people to resist the impression, in view of such problems as pollution, poverty, and urban disintegration, that the liberal assumptions have failed; they have not adequately guided our actions and they have let us in for severe historical disappointments.

Thus I think we must regard the passing of the traditional assumptions both seriously, for it may represent an enduring alteration of attitudes, and hopefully, for—if my criticisms of them are valid—it may show that we are learning. It seems to me appropriate to see a deepening understanding in some of the attitudes displayed by both the New Left and their conservative opponents.

I certainly do not intend these remarks as a blanket endorsement of either side. I would like to think, for example, that young radicals are mistaken in their conviction that the requirements of justice, even in the most complex situations, are perfectly obvious to the young and unspoiled, although they are seldom discerned and respected by their elders; I would like to think that their opponents are mistaken in regarding the nation as so sacred that the individual rarely, if ever, can rightfully resist official demands. Further, not only are the new insights associated at present with much that is false; but it also may turn out to be the false that is triumphant. The danger inherent in the passing of the traditional assumptions was signalized by Fascism. Through that movement, individualism gave way to the violent and systematic destruction of individuals, rationalism was replaced with emotional fury, and the idea of progress was repudiated only to clear the way for mechanized barbarism.

But not everything in our situation—which as a whole is certainly confused and ominous—is discouraging. Dangerous as the breaking up of the liberal consensus is, it cannot be a purely tragic event, if the criticisms I have made are valid. And exaggerated and unattractive as the utterances of groups on the left and right sometimes are, the attitudes they represent do not appear to be altogether unwholesome. Everything depends on whether we can keep our balance, that is, on whether we can acknowledge the inadequacies of liberalism without becoming contemptuous of the decencies for which it stood, and on whether in formulating the new insights that seem to be available we can eliminate hysteria and speak with care for truth and respect for persons.

What are the new insights? They can be summarily defined under three headings that correspond to the criticisms above.

1   *Communalism*   The dissimilarity and separateness of individuals are not accepted either as facts or as values. Whether through the small, democratic groupings desired by the left, or through nation and culture, as the conservatives understand them, we are (using the words of a figure who could not readily be identified with either the left of the right—Paul the Apostle) "members one of another."

2   *Transrationalism*   The more common term "irrationalism" is objectionable on two grounds: it is pejorative, and it suggests the complete rejection of reason. "Transrationalism" simply denotes the idea that reason is insufficient for understanding reality, although possibly helpful. Both Plato's defense of poetic insight and Augustine's reliance on faith are kinds of transrationalism. Examples from more recent times are Rousseau's appeal to the conscience of the common man, reiterated by the New Left, and Burke's praise of tradition, which established one of the main tenets of contemporary conservatism.

3   *Historical pessimism*   Man is looked on as being, at least temporarily if not in all possible circumstances, morally unreliable. The historical pessimism of the left is characteristically expressed in analyses of the shrewd and relentless selfishness of capitalists and politicians (although the pessimism of the left must be regarded as only provisional, in view of the ultimate hopes leftists customarily entertain); that of the right, in warnings of the threat to order and decency posed by idealists who wish quickly to construct a perfect society.

These are very brief definitions but will, perhaps, suffice for the moment in order to clarify the theoretical position we have reached. More complete and exact definitions will be set forth in the following chapter in order to explore the implications of these ideas for tolerance.

I shall not try to offer a systematic defense of communalism, transrationalism, and historical pessimism. To do so would require much more than an essay on tolerance. Our task is to determine the bearing of these general views on the idea of tolerance. Such an analysis offers possibilities, I believe, not only of placing tolerance on firmer theoretical foundations than it rests on at present but also of understanding tolerance anew—of seeing it, indeed, as the principal component of the civility we seem to be in danger of losing but on which the very continuance of historical life may depend.

The three insights cited above are not really new, although they may be counted as discoveries in the context of recent history. They are set forth in various forms in the political writings of ancient Greece; they are found in the New Testament; and in both their Greek and Christian embodiments they passed into the Middle Ages. Political theories embodying all three ideas were formulated late in the eighteenth century and gathered numerous followers. Since then, many writers have in varying ways and degrees expressed communal, transrational, and historically pessimistic attitudes. Thus it would be possible to regard liberalism as only temporarily interrupting the rule of a tradition to which we are now returning.

That the new viewpoints are not unprecedented, however, does not much lessen the dangers of our situation. We may feel respect for ages in which individualism, rationalism, and historical optimism were not so powerful as they have been in recent centuries. But for the most part those were not very tolerant ages; and in any case we cannot return to them. Regardless of how deeply we may revere certain preceding periods, or how extensively we may borrow from them, we still have to create our own visions and our own social forms.

The central question of this essay is whether in doing this we can continue to be tolerant. On the face of things, it is not clear that we can. On the contrary, the new assumptions seem to lend support to the intolerance of both the New Left and the conservatives; they provide a vantage point from which it seems only sensible to condemn the detachment and permissiveness associated with tolerance. Consider, for example, the way things have looked from the point of view of the New Left.

First, given an awareness of human interdependence and a consequent tendency to examine society in its totality rather than to break it down into separate individuals, intolerable extremes of privilege and deprivation have become visible, and the helplessness of individual victims, so long as they remain unorganized and divided, has become apparent. In contrast, individualists of the older tradition paid relatively little attention to the over-all structure of society and tended to leave each individual to take care of himself; their tolerance thus was seemingly of a piece with a complacent acquiescence in injustice. Second, the transrationalistic moral convictions of the New Left have inspired demands for the immediate rectification of wrongs; rationalistic liberals, however, have often seemed willing to prolong study and discussion indefinitely. Finally to the (provisional) historical pessimists of the New Left it has seemed that the spontaneous course of history is unreliable and that justice consequently has to be extracted through organized pressure and perhaps through violence—thus through some kind of intolerance. The historical optimists of the liberal tradition, on the other hand, anticipated that through tolerance the evils in society would be disclosed and corrected, and in this way, more or less detached and inactive, they were apt to fall back on what was assumed to be the spontaneously progressive forces of history. In sum, traditional tolerance depended in some measure on a blindness induced by individualism, rationalism, and historical optimism. Having given up these assumptions, the New Left has seen society and its stubborn injustices afresh. Tolerance has dissolved with the illusions on which it was based.

The intolerance of their conservative opponents, however, is no less reasonable. Radical students have been outraged by efforts to regulate their styles of hair and dress and have vehemently insisted on their freedom to organize and to speak. Their libertarian mood, however, would be more appropriate if they accepted the traditional assumptions. If each one is, and ought to be, more or less separate from everyone else, if people are rational, and if the course of events is spontaneously progressive, then to regulate styles of personal deportment or political activity is as absurd as students have held it to be. If, however, we are "members one of another," if clashing ideas cannot be counted on to open the way to truth, and if men are untrustworthy and order fragile, then the intolerance that outrages the radical students is not so absurd after all. In the 1960s, long hair on a man, for example, was not merely a private matter if regarded from the communal point of view; it expressed a certain attitude toward established society, and it was intended as a form of communication. The students knew this, and it was disingenuous of them to retreat to liberal breastworks when confronted with conservative opponents who understood the significance of their styles.

I hope that I do not make it seem, using such broad strokes as I have, that I am denying that the structure of opinion today contains many variations. For example, as noted above, in economic matters many liberals moved beyond individualism far in advance of the New Left. On the other hand, conservatism has often meant not so much reverence for tradition as rigid adherence to some of the tenets, especially economic individualism, of traditional liberalism. I hope also that I do not seem to be denying the complexities of historical movement. Even if the new understanding is an irresistible tide, it is certain to come in so slowly, and with so many waves that break spectacularly and then recede, that its over-all movement will often be hard to discern.

To deal fully with such variations of opinion and complexities of development, however, would turn this work from a short essay into an extended treatise. And it would, I think, lead us finally to the position we have already reached: that tolerance today rests on views that are dubious and widely rejected, and that it therefore cannot survive, and perhaps does not deserve to, unless it can be placed on new foundations. Tolerance needs to be resituated. It seems to me that political thought in our time has no more important task than finding out whether this is possible.

My own position is not wholly detached. I am biased on the side of tolerance, even though the traditional arguments supporting it seem to me weak. My emotional response to the intolerance of the radicals and of their conservative opponents is one of indignation, despite my having to admit that their intolerance is not altogether unreasonable. Hence the following discussion is aimed at defending tolerance but at defending it on different grounds than those it has rested on in the past. I propose to set aside the individualism, rationalism, and historical optimism of traditional liberalism, to adopt the opposing postulates, and to see whether in that intellectual situation tolerance is defensible.

I remind the reader, however, of earlier disclaimers. Resituating tolerance is too large a task for any one thinker and in particular for the author of this essay. I shall be satisfied if I can sketch some plausible outlines.

II Why Should Men Be Tolerant?

TOLERANCE AND COMMUNITY

1

THE FIRST QUESTION to be considered is whether tolerance is undermined if individualism is replaced with a communal conception of human relations. What happens to tolerance if we give up the idea that each individual can live much of his life in a purely personal sphere where he can be different from all others and where his thoughts and acts have little or no effect on others? What happens to tolerance if we cease thinking that a wise person would wish to inhabit such a sphere even if it were accessible?

It seems to me that tolerance does not collapse under such circumstances and that the intolerance of certain radicals and conservatives is not a necessary consequence of their communalism. Of course, everything depends on precisely how community is defined; it has been defined by both the Left and the Right in ways that preclude tolerance. A proposed definition at odds with typical views of both radicals and conservatives (as well as with the typical individualism of the center) will be a decisive part of the argument that follows. Some readers may well reject my concept of community. However, the argument may help even those who disagree with me, to reflect on the relationship of tolerance and community. I hope it will lead some readers to the conclusion that tolerance is not merely the relic of an individualistic past but must have a place in any future that is authentically communal, and not merely highly organized or fanatically nationalistic.

To argue for this conclusion is not merely to cling to an old value. Tolerance becomes in some measure a new value when the arguments supporting it are altered. The typical concept of community also is changed when it is construed as essentially tolerant. Thus I think my argument suggests a new way of looking at human relations—a way that transcends the old ideologies but is not simply one additional ideology.

At the outset, two points must be made concerning the intellectual background of the present discussion. The first, made in fairness to Mill, is that the essay *On Liberty* manifests many impulses toward a more communal view of things than that of traditional liberalism. It is clear, for example, that Mill thought of individuality as being of great value not just to the individual himself but to society as a whole. In other words, in the very realization of his uniqueness man is playing a communal role. Further, Mill's essay contains many signs that he was aware of human interdependence. As has already been pointed out, he was fully cognizant of the fact that ideas are often extinguished with force, and in this way he showed an awareness of the social character of belief. He did so as well in more than one statement like the following: "Never when controversy avoided the subjects which are large and important enough to kindle enthusiasm, was the mind of a people stirred up from its foundations, and the impulse given which raised even persons of the most ordinary intellect to something of the dignity of thinking beings." [1] That sentence could not have been written by an unqualified individualist.

Mill's communal insights nevertheless remain encased in an extreme and explicit individualism. The major theme of the essay *On Liberty*, stated emphatically and repeatedly, is that a large and inviolable portion of each individual's life is made up of "self-regarding" acts; Mill could not have drawn out the consequences of the communalism that occasionally appears in his writing without capsizing that theme. The notion that individuality is of value to society, for example, implies that none of the thoughts, tastes, and acts that constitute individuality are really self-regarding. *On Liberty* foreshadows the idea of tolerance as a communal stance but never explicitly reaches such an idea.

The second point to be made concerning the intellectual background of the problem under consideration is that criticism of Mill's individualism is far from novel. It was voiced in Mill's own day, not just by people like Thomas Carlyle who were out of sympathy with practically all of Mill's ideas, but by liberals who wished to reconcile liberty and community.

The outstanding figure among these critics was an Oxford professor, Thomas Hill Green. [2] Through studying Hegel, and also through witnessing the effects of industrialization on people's lives, Green realized that the individual is involved in society much more fully and inescapably than was granted in a philosophy like Mill's. Nor did Green consider such involvement necessarily undesirable. He did, however, quite legitimately infer that freedom could not be gained by establishing a sphere in which the individual could live apart from society. Since man was inevitably and properly a social being, freedom depended on organizing society so that individuals had roles that enabled them to realize their potentialities; freedom had to be construed as action within society rather than apart from society. Green was both a sensitive man and a skilled philosopher, and his critique of liberal individualism is generally agreed to be an important chapter in the history of political philosophy.

Nevertheless, some elements are lacking in Green's thought which cannot easily be specified or added together but are likely to be important to anyone concerned with tolerance. Green paid little attention to expression as distinguished from action or to communication as distinguished from other kinds of social relations. He was not nearly as suspicious of society as was Mill, nor was he as appreciative of the originality and courage it takes for an individual to oppose society. Freedom does not seem to have been the spiritual adventure for Green that it was for Mill, despite the spiritual concerns that animated Green's metaphysics; the practical upshot of his thought was that the individual must normally devote himself wholeheartedly to the social roles allotted him by fate. Hence Green may be charged with neglecting tolerance and equating community with society. In consequence, although Green was decidedly superior to Mill in philosophical acumen, it is Mill who stands out as the greater exponent of tolerance.

In sum, the notion of tolerance as a communal attitude is foreshadowed in Mill's writings but is not fully developed even by the critics of his individualism. Thus, the idea of tolerance remains within a doctrinal framework separating it from the idea of community—at least, so far as political philosophers are concerned.

Tolerance is also opposed to community so far as common sense is concerned. Unless I greatly misinterpret prevailing attitudes, tolerance still is derived primarily from what is taken to be the right of the individual to live his own separate life. The strongest defenders of tolerance are apt to be liberals who, outside the sphere of economics, retain much of the individualism of Locke and Mill. The ultimate good gained through tolerance, they assume, is the freedom of the individual to live and think as he pleases. If he harms no one else, his life and thoughts are his own affair. These are maxims of present-day common sense, and they are very much like the individualistic ground principles of Mill's essay.

If tolerance is commonly linked with individualism, the word "community" brings to the minds of most people qualities such as cohesion, uniformity, and discipline: qualities presumed to be antithetical to tolerance. And it is not only liberals, loyal to the principles of Locke and Mill, and unmoved by the communal rhetoric of radicals, who link community and intolerance. Partisans of the notion of community do this as well. Rousseau is a good example. For him, a society that merely assured each citizen the right to live as he pleased—Locke's and Mill's ideal—would leave its members miserable, although it might also render them so decadent as to be unaware of their misery. Men could be virtuous and happy, Rousseau thought, only if their lives were thoroughly shared. If Mill's vision of a good society is represented by a cluster of contiguous circles, Rousseau's may be appropriately symbolized by one large circle. To what extent Rousseau believed in freedom for individuals is a matter of dispute among scholars. The shadows of intolerance cast by many of his ideas, however, are apparent to most readers. He held that human activities, such as education, religious worship, and recreation, should so far as possible be carried on under the observation and control of the public. [3]

At the same time, he felt that extensive discussion of public issues was undesirable, for the needs of society should be readily apparent to everyone. He was also hostile to pressure groups and political parties, on the grounds that they entail division and conflict. At the close of his major work on politics, *The Social Contract*, Rousseau proposed a "censorial tribunal" and a "civil religion"; in relation to the latter, he urged the death penalty for apostasy, even if it were only implied by someone's behavior rather than explicitly announced. [4] The societies Rousseau most admired were ancient Sparta and Republican Rome.

Radical students in recent times have seemed much less enthusiastic than was Rousseau about the kind of discipline typified by Sparta and early Rome. Communal life as they have seen it is far more carefree than it was for Rousseau (who was inspired not only by Sparta and Rome but also by Calvinistic Geneva). The students, however, have shown themselves to be little more tolerant than Rousseau. It is true that their large gatherings, such as peace rallies, have often been impressively pacific; but at such gatherings all participants are presumed to be like-minded. In political disputation, the bearing of radical students has usually been fiercely arrogant, and their aim has been to crush rather than answer their opponents.

At the risk of oversimplification, the problem of resituating tolerance may be conceived as a problem of alliances among ideas. Two old alliances—between individualism and tolerance, and between communality and intolerance—must be dissolved. A new alliance, between communality and tolerance, must be formed. Accomplishing this, as I have suggested, depends on carefully defining community, for I believe that if community is accurately understood it will be apparent that there can be no community without tolerance.

2

Almost everyone who uses the term "community" intends thereby to designate a kind of interpersonal unity that is somehow authentic as distinguished from various kinds of interpersonal unity that are merely apparent. Common conceptions of community have been heavily influenced by Ferdinand Tonnies' well-known distinction between *Gemeinschaft* and *Gesellschaft*.[5] *Gemeinschaft* is "real and organic life," *Gesellschaft* "imaginary and mechanical structure."[6] The former term is typified by an intimate family, the latter by a factory. What is important for our purposes is not the precise nature of the distinction—in my opinion, it is misleading—but the idea that *Gemeinschaft* is conceived to be inherently good ("the expression bad Gemeinschaft violates the meaning of the word"), whereas *Gesellschaft*, although possibly useful, is alien ("One goes into Gesellschaft as one goes into a strange country").[7] Today, following this usage, community seems ordinarily to be thought of as the negation of society. Society is cold and rational, community passionate; society is vast, community small; society is hierarchical, community egalitarian; society is bureaucratic, community personal; and so forth. The concept of community expresses modern man's alienation. It symbolizes a non-alienated life and would probably be incomprehensible apart from its counterconcept, society, which stands for the collective order that imposes alienation.

The concept of community thus has to be handled cautiously. It has a weighty and diverse emotional content, but a weak and indefinite rational form. It can readily be used to express impotent resentment or to justify capricious rebellion. It does, however, represent a widespread and irrepressible sense of distress; it has arisen from the consciousness of countless individuals that they are not at home in the societies they inhabit. Perhaps there has never been a community, in the sense of an empirically identifiable grouping in which the members are authentically united. But even if the concept refers to nothing actual, it still belongs in our thinking as an ideal and as a standard for criticizing the actual.

The central notion in the following argument is that community must be understood through the concept of communication. Community, it may be said, is that which is realized in the activity of communication. Surprisingly, community and communication are not often linked in this way. A community is usually thought of as an association so undifferentiated and so suffused with common feeling that communication—an activity presupposing some distance among persons and the use of reason—would hardly be necessary. In thinking of such an association, however, one is forced to think of its members as having no distinctive and important personal concerns and no capacity or inclination to engage in critical thought. That is why it seems to me that the usual concept of community is erroneous and that one must conceive of this ideal in terms of communication. Through communication, persons associate with one another as independent and rational beings.

The significance of this definition, in the present context, is that communication clearly depends on tolerance. People cannot speak to one another truthfully unless they have freedom. Where community is conceived of as an intimate affective association, tolerance is not implied; in that kind of association there is nothing to be tolerated. If community is what is realized through communication, however, there can be no community without tolerance.

This is the gist of the case for tolerance on communalist grounds. I offer it, however, only to help the reader keep his bearings in the course of the argument that follows. The idea that community requires tolerance and that the purpose of tolerance is communication seems to me novel and important enough to need working out with some care. That is what I shall try to do in the following pages. What seems to be called for, above all, is a full and accurate definition of community; only this will enable us to establish a link between community and tolerance.

Even the more emotional and indefinite uses of the term "community" provide us with a clue as to what community is. It is an association, it is commonly thought, in which one is altogether at home. What help does this metaphor provide? We must ask why home is appealing. The reason, it seems, is that at home one does not have to guard his conduct and attitudes; one can be fully and spontaneously himself. We are led in this way to the idea that a community is an association in which every member, rather than having to sacrifice selfhood for the sake of relationships, can realize his own full being. We experience what this means in personal love, where the relationship brings amplification of being. Let us say, then, that when two or more persons are fully together by virtue of those qualities that make them what they really are, they constitute a community. Or, more concisely: community is the unity of a number of persons in their essential being.

Thus, to read one of the Platonic dialogues that depict Socrates discussing a matter as serious as friendship or justice, with persons who know that the subject is serious and want to discover the truth about it, is to sense that one is reading a drama concerning community—a small and ephemeral community, but an association in which human beings are present to one another as the beings they really are. Whether a Socratic dialogue really does depict community depends of course on whether men are essentially philosophical inquirers. In any case, the idea that man is essentially philosophical and inquiring is plausible enough for the Socratic dialogue to exemplify the definition. On the other hand, a prison might serve as an example of a non-communal association. The inmates of a prison do make up a close and relatively enduring group; the reason they do not constitute a community is not hard to discover: man is not essentially a prisoner. A prisoner may have betrayed his essence through the crime that led to his being imprisoned, but the fact remains that as a prisoner much of his essential being—his freedom, his rationality, his vocational potentialities, and so forth—is unrealized. He is an unwilling and fragmentary participant in the association to which he belongs. It is unpleasantly easy to think of many other associations, such as factories and armies, that are rarely communal.

The definition of community as the unity of men in their essence accords with the emotions that have given rise to the concept of community. People have been preoccupied with community because of their sense that the associations to which they belong compel them to neglect or suppress qualities so important that their elimination is more than painful; it is personally destructive.

Such associations are made up of distorted and incomplete beings. The demand for community expresses a longing for an association in which one remains, or even finds, himself.

So far, however, this definition sheds little light on tolerance. The concept of community as the unity of persons in their essence is too general for that. Hence the concept must be made more specific.

It may seem that this requires a definition of man's essence. That would no doubt be a natural step to take. It would not be an easy step, however. Defining man's essence in a way that would meet with general assent, thus providing a secure basis for the theory of tolerance would be so difficult that one naturally looks about for a less perilous route on which to advance. Further, there is the question as to whether man even has an essence in the same sense in which a desk or a tree, or any other entity in the world, has an essence. The source of this question—which has been extensively developed in existentialist literature—is that in the very act of defining his essence man transcends it and puts himself in a position to depart from it in his life. It is possible to conclude that man's essence is chosen, or even created, by man himself.

At later stages in these reflections, this subject will come more fully to light. At the present stage, however, it seems unnecessary to wrestle with the difficulties it involves. There is, I think, a way of passing around them. The procedure I propose to follow is that of trying to define—not the human essence itself, but—certain qualities that must be present in man if that essence is to be realized. Concerning the characteristics of man's essence and its ontological status (that is, whether or not it is created by man himself), nothing need be said. What will be done instead is to indicate certain conditions without which a human being cannot be authentically himself; these conditions are human qualities—qualities, I believe, that people with diverse views of man's essence might agree are indispensable for the realization of that essence.

By following this procedure, the requirements of the inquiry should be satisfied. Some insight should be gained into the nature of community, for if community is the realization of the human essence in oneself and others, then it necessarily involves acceptance of the qualities in oneself and others on which that realization depends. Such insight may, if we are fortunate, enable us to decide on the general relationship of community and tolerance.

I suggest that there are two qualities of the kind we are looking for. I believe that each of these qualities can best be designated by using a common word but by giving that word a meaning somewhat different from that in daily usage. The first quality to be considered may be termed "veracity."

The meaning this term discloses on analysis, and the one that I wish to make use of here is in two ways more complex than the meaning it is apt to have in casual conversation. To begin with, when we attribute veracity to someone, we usually mean merely that he can be relied on to tell the truth—a simple trait because telling the truth is considered no more than a matter of honesty. To be a reliable spokesman for the truth, however, it is not enough to be honest; one must know what the truth actually is. We cannot legitimately attribute veracity to someone who is perpetually confused; it is doubtful even that we can legitimately attribute veracity to someone who is ignorant and confesses his ignorance. In short, veracity is truthfulness, and truthfulness requires not only honesty but understanding as well.

Further, the "veracity" of common usage is a quality that characterizes relationships; when we speak of veracity we think of two or more persons, not of a single, solitary person. If we pause to reflect, however, we will realize that someone who has for a long time had no occasion to speak truthfully to anyone else—a prisoner kept in solitary confinement, for example, or a disaffected subject of a totalitarian regime—might nevertheless be veracious. This shows that veracity is primarily a relationship not with others but with oneself. To be veracious, I must tell the truth to myself; only then am I in a position to tell the truth to others.

This brings into view a variety of psychological complexities. We all know, for example, that even when a person understands the truth he may refuse to "face" it and may tell himself something else that he would prefer to believe. Moreover, it seems likely that a failure of honesty in relation to others often stems from an act of self-deceit. If this is so, then the Machiavellian idea that a ruler must clearly see the truth but be prepared to lie about it prescribes a more difficult feat of psychological acrobatics than readers of Machiavelli often realize; if one is effectively to deceive others, his life will be far simpler and more easily managed if he can first deceive himself. Hence the astonishment we feel in finding someone in a "bare-faced lie."

Veracity, then, is a matter of telling the truth—to others if possible, to oneself without fail. Why is this a condition of realizing one's essential being? Presumably everyone would grant that veracity is usually admirable, but many might doubt that it is a prerequisite of selfhood.

Two mutually consistent answers can be given, and both seem to me to be true. One of them, however, is more readily understandable and more generally acceptable than the other. To note the more understandable and acceptable answer first, one who is lacking in veracity cannot become cognizant either of his own potentialities or of the conditions governing their actualization. Granted, the self is something that is chosen; yet it is chosen from a limited range of possibilities. What I am to be, I must choose, but I cannot choose anything I please. My alternatives are limited both by my personal qualities and by my situation. A middle-aged professor cannot choose to become an outstanding athlete; that is manifest. It is not so manifest, however, whether he can choose to become an outstanding writer; here a nice weighing of individual potentialities and surrounding conditions is required. It is this kind of weighing that places demands on veracity. Only with veracity can selfhood be chosen realistically.

I suggest further that even the self one chooses must first be discovered—that one chooses not arbitrarily but in response to a sense that he has discerned what in some sense he really is. This is the second, and more difficult and disputable, answer to the question, Why is veracity a prerequisite of selfhood? It presents a paradoxical notion, but one that is often accepted by common sense. An example is offered by the amount of attention given nowadays to the problem of identity, of "finding out who you really are." And is not the inseparability of selfhood and veracity recognized when someone is praised for being "natural," in the sense of being unaffected? If choosing oneself were purely arbitrary, then all selfhood would be affectation. In condemning affectation, however, we recognize that the self that is chosen is not necessarily the "true self." The possibility of a contrary view is shown by philosophies such as Sartre's, in which one's nature is construed as a decree of absolute, unguided freedom; the self does not precede, but is a product of, that primal freedom. In the last analysis, however, such philosophies usually, if not always, distinguish in some way between the right kinds and the wrong kinds of choices; they often, for example, develop a concept such as Martin Heidegger's notion of "authenticity." Thus the "true self" is readmitted after being initially excluded.

Questions concerning the nature of the self that must be discovered prior to being chosen need not be considered here. I do not want to tie the concept of veracity to any particular ontological or moral theory, such as natural law. As I have already noted, whether man has a nature, in the same sense in which a tree has a nature, and whether, if he does, that nature possesses moral authority, are difficult and unresolved issues, and we need not become involved in them in the present inquiry. The essential self may be universal and rationally comprehensible, as in natural law, or inherently undefinable, as is *Existenz* in the philosophy of Karl Jaspers; it may be subject to systematic investigation and control, or it may be at the disposal of God alone. My argument is simply that one cannot be that essential self without understanding and honesty—without veracity.

All that needs to be added concerning veracity is that its subject matter should not be narrowly construed. One must, of course, try to understand one's potentialities and personal situation, but that is not all. A person is perhaps less a thing than a certain perspective. If we are fully to describe a person, we must characterize his views and convictions in general, not just so far as they concern himself; and even when we specify his occupation, place of residence, family situation, and so forth, we are describing the angle from which he apprehends the world. A person might be largely identified (not fully—that would leave choice out of account) in terms of the world as he sees it, in terms, that is, of *his* truth. What one believes even about the stars bears on his selfhood (consider, for example, the issue of astrology). Every notion that I accept as truth becomes an element in my own being. Hence, while veracity is in one sense a relationship with myself (telling myself the truth), in another sense it is a relationship with all of reality (telling myself the *whole* truth).

In the course of this discussion, we have repeatedly had to recognize that choice is somehow involved in selfhood, and in doing this we have acknowledged the second quality, in addition to veracity, that is required for selfhood. This quality may conveniently be termed "responsibility."

In ordinary usage, responsibility means being held accountable for one's conduct. One may be held accountable by a particular body or person, as an elected representative is to his constituents, or one may be held accountable to oneself, as we grant when we speak of someone "holding himself responsible." Let us accept established usage to the extent of saying that a responsible person is somehow subject to the demand that he "explain himself"—that he explain his act of self-choice or some aspect of that act. Let us depart somewhat from established usage, however, and specify that the primary author of this demand must be oneself. Like veracity, responsibility is first of all a relationship a person establishes with himself. Someone might be aware of ways in which he is negligent and malicious, of failures and cruelties in his past behavior, of which it would be inappropriate to try to give anyone else a full accounting. That person still might be called "responsible" if he were regularly to provide *himself* with a full accounting—an accounting that in no way minimizes or unjustifiably excuses the evils contained within it. That accounting would constitute the internal structure that is the substance of responsibility. However, if one were somehow to give others an accurate accounting (when drunk, for example) that he never had given, and never would give, to himself, we would not call him responsible.

As noted above, the imperative of responsibility derives from freedom. Although selfhood must be discovered, it also must be chosen. To be responsible, however, is not simply to be free. As Sartre has so effectively argued, man is condemned to be free. One is not, however, condemned to be responsible: responsibility is more than freedom. It is a relationship with one's freedom—a relationship one may (freely) refuse. The nature of that relationship is implied by the initial definition of responsibility offered above. One is responsible when the use he makes of his freedom is a matter concerning which he is prepared to give an accounting.

The relations of responsibility to veracity present a large and complex topic, but one that need not delay us here. Responsibility lies in an attitude toward one's freedom; veracity, in an attitude toward reality. The standard of responsibility is the good, or the right, that of veracity the true. Responsibility depends on veracity; surely, one of the most indisputable lessons of psychoanalysis is that internal battles cannot be successfully fought without self-understanding and honesty. On the other hand, sustained veracity, in which the hardest truths are lucidly faced, is not likely to be achieved without responsibility; thus the order of dependence runs in both directions. All of this is sketchy in the extreme, but to try to be more complete and systematic would unnecessarily detain us.

The concept of responsibility involves one difficulty, however, that bears sufficiently on the central concerns of this essay to require somewhat more extended consideration. That difficulty stems from the negative position taken above in relation to the ideal of personal uniqueness.

I have argued that uniqueness would not be a feasible goal, even if it were a desirable one, owing to such conditions as the relative inflexibility of personality structure and the impossibility of objectively comprehending that structure. These limits render every person in large degree a social type. It may seem, however, that if uniqueness must be ruled out on these grounds, responsibility must be ruled out as well. For if society imposes certain general characteristics on its members, each individual is inevitably left with little say. How, then, can we speak of responsibility?

It seems to me a decisive fact in relation to this question that, while one can hardly escape being representative of his society, there are different ways of being representative. It is not only Socrates who embodied Athenian character; so did Alcibiades. There are profound and creative, as well as reckless and destructive, ways of being the general type of human being that one is bound to be. Perhaps not every human being is free to choose between such heights and depths as those symbolized by Socrates and Alcibiades. It does seem plain, however, that the uniformity inherent in the very existence of society does not foreclose the issues of morality. Although similarity and uniqueness are not real alternatives for an individual, good and evil are.

But is this not to embrace an exaggerated conception of the scope of freedom—a conception of the very sort that was rejected in criticizing the ideal of uniqueness? Not necessarily, for it can be argued that one departs from a standard set by society only by appealing to another. Consider, for example, someone who is assuming responsibility for himself by trying to reform his own character. Such efforts depend on an example or an ideal found in society. One can rebel against certain examples or ideals, but such rebellion can hardly be sustained, and is not likely even to arise, without inspiration and support from counterexamples or counterideals. The moral struggle of the individual, however demanding it may be, is

a struggle to actualize ideals and possibilities presented by the social world around him.

The ideal of uniqueness is vulnerable, however, not only in view
of the limits of imagination and strength that force the individual,
when passing through the ordeals of self-choice, to rely heavily on
society. It can be challenged also on the grounds that a human being cannot transcend himself. He is never in a position to choose
himself with the rationality possible in choosing, say, an automobile or a home. One can stand off from a physical object and examine it objectively and comprehensively; but one cannot do this with
oneself. A person never gains a complete picture of himself but
must, as it were, look at himself first from one side and then from
another. Self-knowledge is inherently fragmentary because the
known object must serve as knowing, and hence unknown, subject. I do not mean to imply that some things can be totally objec-
tified. Even a stone, in its individual concreteness, is something
more than a mineralogist can know about it; the difference between
a particular concrete human being and a psychologist's theoretical
reconstruction of his personality must be immeasurable. But the
limits of objective knowledge become even narrower in relation
to the self because only here must the same entity serve both as
object and as subject. And this consideration applies with particular force to our present concern, which is that of choosing oneself.
It signifies that in doing this one scarcely knows what one is about.

The result is to enhance the power of society even further. Not
only must one consciously depend on society for moral guidance
and inspiration; and not only does one consciously give way before the pressure of society, as when acquiescing, willingly or not,
in old habits. One is also shaped by society in ways he cannot wholly comprehend; every American is American in ways no amount
of self-analysis will enable him ever to understand. This brings into
view man's subjection to the natural causality that operates
through the social order. So far as I can understand the causes affecting me, I become free of them. Causes that are unrecognized,
however, are necessarily irresistible. Hence it may be said, in sum,
that my weakness before society is not just moral—not just a matter of conscious dependence; it is ontological.

To return momentarily to the basic concepts being developed,
we are discussing here limits on veracity that are necessarily translated into limits on responsibility. The question is whether an

affirmation of the kind of moral freedom symbolized by the polarity of Socrates and Alcibiades flies in the face of this situation.

It seems to me that it does not, for nothing I have said implies the unreality of freedom. What we see, rather, is that freedom is far more limited in scope and uncertain in results than we usually acknowledge. In shaping and choosing himself, a human being may be likened to a sculptor, working with unfamiliar materials, in a darkness only occasionally and partially broken. This is no doubt a less appealing state than most people think of when they speak of freedom, but it is nevertheless freedom. Still, one may ask, how much is it worth?

As much, it might be answered, as the soul which, according to the biblical saying, one would not exchange for the whole world. However limited and blind responsibility may be, it marks the difference between selfhood and mere biological existence. If one did not choose, even within the limits set by his moral weakness and ontological situation, he would not be a person at all but only a set of dispositions and faculties loosely related by their common dependence on a single organism. The self cannot be an established achievement; it is at best an undertaking and a hope. Only through responsibility, however, does one resist the forces tending to reduce one's life to the mere passage of sensations and enter into this undertaking and this hope.

Perhaps this is only to repeat the commonplace that to be human one must be free. Returning to the path of discourse where we were challenged by the question as to whether it is possible to be free, we may ask why it is necessary to be accountable as well.

The answer does not appear complex. Only by holding oneself accountable, I believe, can one choose resolutely and carefully. Of course, a responsible person often, or even usually, discovers that there is no one else to whom he can render an accounting; he remains, then, accountable only to himself. What happens in an instance of this kind is that the individual constitutes himself an imaginary society of two; in the role of one member he renders his accounting, in the role of the other he receives it. This may sound odd, but I believe that most people do it almost continuously, and we recognize this in the name we ordinarily apply to the self that demands and receives the accounting, that is, "conscience."

Let us pause and glance at our over-all position. Our aim is to gain insight into community in order to assess the implications for tolerance of accepting a communal viewpoint. We began by defining community as the unity of a number of persons in their essential being and moved forward by specifying veracity and responsibility as qualities necessary for realizing one's essential being. It has been seen that veracity provides only fitful and uncertain light but that responsibility is not impossible and is not, despite the limits and uncertainties attending it, without decisive bearing on the effort to be human. It should be possible now to say something more about the nature of community, and on that basis perhaps we can draw some conclusions concerning tolerance.

In approaching the matter of community, the first thing to be noted is that our discussion has confirmed one of the basic postulates of this essay—that man is a communal being. Veracity and responsibility are conditions of not only realizing one's essential being but also entering fully into communication. They delineate the state of someone who is available, so to speak, in relation to other persons. This point deserves brief elaboration in connection with each of the two standards.

Veracity, it was said above, is truthfulness with oneself. It is thus a kind of inner communality; and if veracity is a condition of authentic selfhood, this inner communality is a requirement imposed by the very effort to be a person. To be myself, I must become an imaginary community—a place where the truth is told unreservedly. This is a demand upon my solitude. At the same time, however, it points beyond solitude. The relationship I must realize with myself is potentially a relationship with all others; if I am truthful with myself, I am in a position to be truthful with all. Veracity is a communicative relationship with reality; one does not just dumbly apprehend what is but engages in discourse—at least with himself and if possible with others.

Responsibility is also communal. This may be seen by noting how it differs from autonomy—one of the individualistic virtues emphasized by Mill. It is true that a responsible person is autonomous in the sense of being, in some measure, self-chosen. But the concept of responsibility has an added ingredient. Autonomy is going one's own way, while responsibility is being prepared to explain—to respond for—the way one is going. Both autonomy and responsibility are forms of freedom. The former, however, is isolated freedom, whereas the latter is freedom so structured as to constitute a potential relationship—a relationship both with one-self and with others. If veracity is a communicative relationship with reality, responsibility is a communicative relationship with one's freedom; one does not realize his freedom silently but rather in readiness for the kind of discourse involved in rendering an accounting.

This whole discussion has perhaps been gradually bringing us nearer to an understanding of community, and, although little has been said directly about community, I hope that we are somewhat like passengers on a ship slowly approaching a shore at first only dimly and half-consciously seen but suddenly plainly visible before us. Community must be a unity of persons who are veracious and responsible and who have actualized the interpersonal relationships potential in these states of being. Community must come into being when the internal relationships of veracity and responsibility are externalized. What is usually called "communication" may be understood as the outward manifestation of veracity and responsibility. This proposition takes us back to the hypothesis formulated at the outset: that the substance of community is not the all-engulfing emotional or habitual unity that drowns all personal distinctness and all thought but, rather, communication.

Does not such a view explain how community can be founded in communication without being one-sidedly intellectual? The communication that creates community, after all, is concerned with those truths that are seen to bear on the task of being human, and it is weighted with the moral seriousness attendant on accounting for what one has, and has not, become. Its gravity lies in lasting truth and in an accounting that surveys all of history.

But what does this concept of community tell us about tolerance? Can it help us understand the role of tolerance once the postulate of individualism is rejected? I think it can, although the conclusion that emerges is not perfectly simple.

Tolerance is not indispensable for the attainment of veracity and responsibility. We are not allowed to say simply that tolerance is demanded by the conditions of selfhood. An individual may be truthful with himself, and accountable to himself, even though he lives under a government that would not permit him either to speak the truth as he understands it or to account honestly for his own life and character. The tragic history of intellectuals in Russia, to cite one of many examples, has proven this. Generation after generation of Russian men and women have scaled heights of veracity and accountability despite political regimes that responded to these accomplishments with sentences of imprisonment, exile, and death.

But, while tolerance is not absolutely indispensable for realizing one's essential being, surely it helps. It would be contrary to all common sense to suppose that veracity and responsibility are not hindered by regimes that treat them systematically and vindictively as crimes. This is the first argument in behalf of tolerance. As has already been noted, through veracity and responsibility one constitutes an inner community; one is truthful and accountable in relation to oneself. If these relationships cannot be established with other persons, however, one is driven into perilous incongruities. For he who cannot be truthful with those around him must be tempted to cease being truthful with himself, hoping thereby to escape from the insecurity and anguish of systematic deception; and he for whom genuine accountability is barred must find it taxing to sustain responsibility in solitude. Probably the achievements of Russian intellectuals would not have been possible but for the relative ineffectiveness of the Czarist regimes. Russian governments have been ferociously intolerant, but intellectual groups have sometimes been able to create small, precarious spheres of tolerance.

The second argument for tolerance depends less on empirical surmise. Tolerance is unconditionally necessary if veracity and responsibility are to be externalized—if, rather than characterizing the structure of a single personality, they are to characterize interpersonal relations. In other words, while tolerance may not be a necessary condition of the realization of a person's essential being, it is a necessary condition of the disclosure of that being. In speaking of disclosure, we are speaking of communication. These statements indicate the chain that I am trying to forge in the present argument—a chain whose major links are community, communication, and tolerance. Reduced to its simplest terms, there is no community without communication, and no communication without tolerance. Veracity and responsibility constitute the strength of that crucial middle link.

The third argument for tolerance is apt to be somewhat puzzling to the reader, but I am convinced that it is sound and important. Even if permitting others to be veracious and responsible somehow enhanced the difficulties of communication, thus hindering the achievement of community, one would still be obliged to sanction veracity and responsibility. Why? Because these qualities are so indissolubly associated with the essence of man that refusing to recognize them would, entirely apart from other consequences, be disruptive of human relationships. In other words, if I wish to enter into community I must grant others room for veracity and responsibility without consideration of the consequences. Otherwise, I isolate myself at the outset. If community is an end in itself, then recognizing others as potentially veracious and responsible is also an end in itself. The tensions and dislocations of our time oftentimes render the consequences of tolerance uncertain. Hence, if we are to be realistically and tenaciously tolerant, we must beware of relying entirely on results. More will be said in this vein when we try to come to terms with the rejection of historical optimism.

Much of the preceding argument might be restated in terms of the concept of attentiveness. Another person cannot become communally present to me unless he is veracious and responsible; otherwise he is concealed from me in a fog arising from carelessness, or confusion, or affectation. I may try to penetrate that fog, for example by asking questions in Socratic fashion, or even by scoffing at or upbraiding the person concealed in it. But each act of this kind has to be followed by a proffer of attention, by a pause in which I await a response. My attentiveness is an acknowledgement that I cannot force, or in any way deliberately draw, the other person into my company. The most I can do is to be attuned to his appearing. This is to say that I am bound to be tolerant.

One can hardly reflect on attentiveness without wondering whether it has not become, for technological man in his self-confidence and impatience, a difficult and even incomprehensible attitude. If so, then strong tendencies toward intolerance lie at the heart of industrial civilization even where formal liberty is protected.

It will be apparent to the reader that I depart rather widely from prevalent views concerning the nature of community, and that this divergence is essential to my argument. Ordinarily, the word "community" is applied to some particularly cohesive social unit, such as a primitive tribe or an ethnic neighborhood. But a community in this sense may entail little or no communication, if communication is understood as not merely talking idly or exchanging information but as mutual presentation of serious personal concerns.

Of course, communication is not possible where there is no social cohesion; but neither is it possible where the degree of social cohesion is so great that individuals do not have their own distinct concerns and views and where freedom for presenting such concerns and views is lacking. The social conditions favoring tolerance will be discussed in the final chapter of this essay. What is being pointed out here is simply that community, understood as a product of communication, can come into being only with a loosening of social ties. In this sense, community presupposes a degree and kind of alienation.

If this is so, then much that is said about "community" today is of doubtful validity. It can be questioned, for example, whether Tönnies' concept of *Gemeinschaft* has any applicability whatever to genuine community. A society so instinctively and wholly at one as Tönnies seems to envision would tend to preclude veracity and responsibility. Tolerance thus would be superfluous, and communication would be an unlikely occurrence. The nostalgia for tribal and feudal unity that is often expressed by critics of modern society seems to me antithetical not merely to values like freedom and privacy, which such critics may care little about, but to the value they are apt to care most about, that of community.

These considerations explain why totalitarianism and community are incompatible. From the outside, totalitarian nations usually appear to be awesomely united, and one can make the mistake of thinking that by sacrificing freedom they have gained community. Accounts of life within such nations, however, show that in destroying freedom they have destroyed community as well. Their unity is a unity of fragmentary beings, terrorized and cajoled into giving up their essential selves.

The argument sketched above really turns essentially on the elementary notion that nothing deserving the name of "community" can come into existence where people are not free to be and to express themselves. The concepts of veracity and responsibility are intended to show just what this means and why it is so.

For this argument to be clear even in its general outlines, however, it is necessary that its limits be taken explicitly into account. Tolerance is a *necessary* condition of community, but it is not a *sufficient* condition of community. We must take time to reflect on this qualification, for if it is ignored the relationship of tolerance to society at large as well as to social policy is bound to be misunderstood.

3

The proposition that tolerance is a necessary, but not sufficient, condition of community can be explained merely by noting that tolerance may permit the disclosure of a debased and guilty self rather than the essential self toward which it is oriented. That tolerance may open the way for deception and irresponsibility has been illustrated countless times in America, with its deep involvement in profit making. And, even where tolerance meets with veracity and responsibility, these attributes may reveal something other than the essential self; a repentant criminal may, according to the definitions above, be veracious and responsible.

None of this casts doubt on the thesis that tolerance is an indispensable condition of community. What it does do is to open up the possibility that the attainment of community may require, in addition to tolerance, certain non-tolerant measures. For example, community might in some circumstances be furthered by coercive tactics designed to hold a people together. Did not Lincoln contribute to the realization of community in America (so far as this has occurred at all)? Community might be furthered in some circumstances by judicial processes, as when a criminal is led to give an accounting in which his guilt is recognized and the task of transcending it is thus begun. The prospects of community are presumably enhanced by rigorous education of the sort that aims to make students capable of a highly refined veracity that is not, in view of the pedagogical severity it entails, very tolerant. It is not inconceivable, that even censorship, which directly contradicts tolerance, might contribute to community; it might do so, for example, were it directed solely at purveyors of salacious literature designed to exploit freedom of communication for monetary gain.

It may seem, then, that the preceding argument for tolerance does not go very far; it may seem that it falls far short of justifying a tolerant society. Such an impression is, I feel, mistaken, but unless it is corrected with some care, so that neither too little nor too much is claimed for tolerance, the whole bearing of the present argument may be misunderstood.

To begin with, it is quite true that tolerance cannot be the sole principle of public policy. Those liberals who would make tolerance an absolute, to be defended blindly, without considering its relation to the ultimate ends of man, and to other means to those ends, seem to me dogmatists and thus mistaken, even if they are more beneficent than other dogmatists. Noting that tolerance is a necessary but not sufficient condition of community is worthwhile, then, partly because it reminds us that tolerance is merely relative— to the end of community and to other means required by that end. The principle of tolerance does not permit us to dispense with political prudence.

While tolerance is not an absolute, however, neither is it merely one among a number of possible means to community. Every other means must finally give way to tolerance. Thus Lincoln contributed to community partly because his repressive and even unconstitutional devices were wisely designed to preserve a constitution that institutionalized tolerance; judicial processes are conducive to community only if judgment and punishment give way at some point to an openness in which erstwhile judges and criminals await one another as beings who are potentially veracious and responsible; educational rigor cannot accomplish very much unless those subject to it learn attentiveness and openness; and censorship must be destructive of community if it is not confined strictly to the task of helping to keep clear and uncorrupted the channels of communication. The orchestration of such devices, in relation to one another and to tolerance, is a task belonging to statesmen rather than to philosophers. Hence we need not ask exactly when and where non-tolerant measures should be abandoned in favor of tolerance; that is a prudential question. I believe that the preceding arguments have established, however, that the orchestration of policy measures must recognize the ascendancy of tolerance. Tolerance is the final gateway through which everyone must pass in approaching community.

Moreover, it must be recognized that the ascendancy of tolerance cannot mean merely that every non-tolerant activity must at some point be replaced with tolerance. A society cannot be abruptly switched over from repression to tolerance, as though it were a machine. Tolerance needs to be nurtured by time, tradition, and culture. Tolerance must therefore in some way pervade even the non-tolerant activities of society. Thus, to appeal once more to the examples cited above, although Lincoln's major actions during the Civil War were on the whole repressive and violent, Lincoln himself was a man of vast tolerance and patiently bore the most diverse and cutting criticisms throughout the War; and judicial and educational processes seem unlikely to succeed unless they combine, with severity and rigor, an attentive tolerance.

What the principle of tolerance does is to humble man, to deny his mastery. It reminds him that, at least so far as community is concerned, having done all else he must reconcile himself to waiting. This necessity is imposed by the veracity and responsibility on which community depends. A boundary thus is drawn around our powers of action. We can produce an incalculable quantity of things but we cannot produce human beings; and while we can organize human beings we cannot deliberately and assuredly unite them in community. Thus social actions like judging and educating must be limited in aims and tentative in spirit.

Up to this point, I have tried to show that tolerance is not threatened by "communalism" so far as that means simply that community is the highest value. That term was used, however, to refer not only to a value but also to a condition—a uniformity and mutual involvement that, in criticizing Locke and Mill, I held to be unavoidable in view of both man's nature and the prerequisites of community. What we must try to do now is to assess the implications of this aspect of communalism for tolerance.

4

Mill's argument for tolerance (and Locke's too, although Locke was somewhat less explicit) presupposed not only that man seeks a state of individual uniqueness and separateness but that such a state is a possibility inherent in the nature of society. Thus Mill thought that the individual could rise above the influence of others and create his own unique personality; he also thought that in doing this the individual could inhabit a "self-regarding" sphere of life where his acts and thoughts would have little effect on others. Both of these notions were important in his defense of tolerance; only by rising above the influence of others could the individual attain the sort of uniqueness that would need to be tolerated, and only (if Mill's claim that he was founding tolerance on the concept of self-regarding action is accepted at face value) because the individual's conduct had little direct effect on others could tolerance be defended.

As was brought out in the preceding chapter, however, Mill seems considerably to have exaggerated both the possibility and desirability of the uniqueness and separateness he envisioned. The truth seems to be that everyone is predestined to be more or less representative of his society and culture and perhaps also of the universal qualities defining the human species; nor is it clear that such a situation is undesirable. As for Mill's conviction that each person can live in a sphere of self-regarding thoughts and acts, what actually prevails seems to be an interdependence which assures that thoughts and acts important to their author will be important to others as well.

These conditions suggest a state of social solidarity in which any claim to tolerance would be irrelevant, because all persons would be substantially alike, and impracticable, because all individual thoughts and acts would affect others and thus would have to be supervised by society. If these were real implications of the criticisms brought against Mill, it would be necessary to conclude that the rejection of traditional liberal individualism jeopardizes tolerance. That they are not real implications, however, can be shown, I think, by means of the concepts developed in the preceding section. Let us begin by considering the significance of the similarity that is the destiny of human beings.

The challenge inherent in the idea that individuals are inevitably similar is the loss of personal distinctness and reality. If each individual is much like every other individual, it may seem that there can be no occasion for tolerance.

Does not the apparent seriousness of this challenge, however, depend altogether on the assumption that authentic and distinctive selfhood, and uniqueness, are the same? If they are, then all uniformity marks a violation of personality by society and the species. But if genuine personal being requires veracity and responsibility, rather than uniqueness, the challenge is less ominous. Although each person may be more or less representative of his time and place, and of the human species, it is possible to be veraciously and responsibly representative. By reflection and choice, a person can make his own the attitudes, ideas, and fundamental nature he has inherited. Tradition, culture, and law become what they surely must be if they are to possess any value: that is, the grounds for authentic, personal humanity.

Let me return to the example of Socrates. Socrates' life work, it can be said, was to question the fundamental beliefs of his countrymen; the questioning went on for decades. During this time, Socrates practiced a recognized craft in Athens, fought with Athenian armies, worshipped the deities of the city, and obeyed the laws even when they decreed his own death. It does not appear that he was trying to become anything other than a representative and loyal Athenian. His goal was apparently to illuminate rationally the social order that he embodied and to do this for the purpose not of being unique but of realizing his humanity reflectively and freely. Socrates manifested an unassuming but relentless veracity and, a stubborn responsibility, as on the occasion when he ignored a governmental order that he regarded as illegal. The result was not that he was divested of his typically Athenian and universally human characteristics but that these became the substance of his personal being.

I do not assume that uniqueness is wholly impossible. Every person, no doubt, is in certain ways unique; and veracity and responsibility may sometimes eventuate in a high degree of uniqueness. Social conditions must have an influence in this matter. A society embodying diverse groups and points of view, and allowing its members to become acquainted with past and foreign cultures, provides relatively large opportunities for uniqueness. Ancient Athens was such a society; one could be a supporter of the many or of the few (a "leftist" or a "conservative"), listen to teachers representing various philosophical viewpoints, and talk to sailors and traders from other parts of the world. No doubt some unusual personalities made their appearance.

My argument has been in part that the possibilities for uniqueness are much more restricted than is generally recognized. To become a unique personality is not within the capacity of most people—perhaps it is not really an option open to anyone. We necessarily follow patterns and examples, and usually we cannot understand and intelligently conform to any that do not come from our own, or from a culturally allied, nation.

What particularly concerns us at this point, however, is not the possibility of uniqueness but its value. Here again, I do not intend to take an absolutely unqualified position; I do not assume that uniqueness is wholly without value. It seems to enter in some way into creativity and also into historical development; and personal uniqueness may no doubt serve at least as a heartening symbol of veracity and responsibility. But I believe that the value of uniqueness, like its possibility, is more limited than is generally assumed.

Considering first the apparent link between uniqueness and creativity, it must be granted that it is difficult to envision the latter in the absence of the former. However, the degree to which creativity has been glorified, even by outstanding thinkers such as Nicolai Berdyaev, can be questioned. It is striking how sharply, the artist and the saint are distinguished, both in traditional evaluations and in historical actuality; creativity and moral pre-eminence seem rarely to coincide in one person. Aside from this consideration, the uniqueness of a work of art may be one of its most superficial characteristics; when we are deeply moved by a creative work, we are far more likely to speak of its "depth" or its "universality" than of its uniqueness.

As for the role of uniqueness in historical progress, the commonplace assumption that new developments are originated by unique personalities and consolidated by conforming multitudes is probably an oversimplification and may be altogether wrong. We really do not know how history develops. Perhaps the insights that prompt historical development make their way first into the minds of the multitudes and are only articulated by leading figures. Or, if history does depend on unique personalities, it is possible that those personalities, far from setting a general standard for everyone, are evil. This is suggested by the myth of Cain and Abel, as well as by the story of Romulus and Remus.

In other respects, it is hard to see that uniqueness has much value except as a possible sign of the lucidity and freedom we have been considering (and these qualities are not necessarily manifest in uniqueness). Veracity and responsibility might lead a person to conform to a certain human type or even to behave as multitudes around him are behaving, whereas uniqueness might come from capriciousness or vanity. The universal and the common are sometimes good; kindness and mutual care are universally approved, and during World War II, for example, courage and patience were commonplace among the people of Great Britain. Uniqueness, on the other hand, is sometimes evil; there are unique crimes and u-unique diseases. It is sometimes impersonal; there are unique rocks and unique clouds. At its roots, a unique personality may be misanthropic and irritable. In the concept of eccentricity we recognize the moral neutrality, if not the moral dubiousness, of uniqueness as such.

What I seek so far as my own being is concerned, and so far as I am true to the most compelling imperatives I am aware of, is not to be different from everyone else but to be deeply and authentically myself. The self I seek to realize, the loss of which would

mean the loss of all I care about, is perhaps most accurately designated by the word "soul"—a word with connotations of neither
similarity nor uniqueness. Sometimes, it is true, I feel that I am
lost if I do what all others are doing, and that conformity is a kind
of damnation; but in other circumstances (say, if I am an English-
man during World War II) it may be my duty to conform. If we
can break through the sentimentality and vulgarity that have come
to surround the word "soul," and think of the reality it signifies
as seriously as did Socrates or some of the early Christians, we will
perceive the absurdity of characterizing the soul in terms either of
uniqueness or of similarity. The word directs our attention to a
dimension of being in which such categories seem to have little
relevance.

Statements of this kind are equally valid, I believe, in relation
to others. What repels us more than anything else is superficiality
or falseness—a sign that someone either has not recognized or is
unwilling to disclose the being he fundamentally is; we are repelled,
in short, by the absence of veracity and responsibility. What at-
tracts us is something certainly more mysterious than uniqueness.
The modern philosopher who has spoken of this reality most powerfully, Martin Buber, has called it simply the "Thou." Here particularly, we can feel the irrelevance of comparisons. Uniqueness
is determined by a comparison that must be made in a state of detachment; awareness of the "Thou" depends on the disappearance
of the separate, observant "I." Uniqueness is discerned by standing
off from someone and seeing him alongside others. The "Thou"—
one who is loved, or even, momentarily, one who is seriously addressed—"fills the sky," as Buber has said. In love and communication, comparisons have little importance.

The impossibility of equating personality and uniqueness becomes apparent in contemplating a great personality of the past.
Abraham Lincoln may serve as an example. Certainly, given the
strangeness and grandeur of his personality, there has been no one
like him among the world's statesmen; and, considering the way
he towered over his time, it seems valid to say that there was no
one like him in nineteenth-century America. Yet to characterize
him simply as unique would seem inept and superficial. One cannot begin to describe his greatness without speaking of his com-
monness—of the fact that he seemed deeply to share the thoughts
and feelings of ordinary Americans of his age.

Tolerance opens the doors to personal being. This seems to be the chief point—a point that the concept of uniqueness may have been intended to make but that in some ways, at least, it obscures. Seeing uniqueness as the main manifestation of personality risks the degradation of personality to mere eccentricity; likewise, defending tolerance in terms of so subordinate a value as uniqueness invites the conclusion that tolerance itself is of subordinate importance. The full significance of tolerance becomes apparent only when it is seen as openness between persons, readiness for relationships.

It may be asked what there is to tolerate other than uniqueness. The answer in part is *social* differences. Mill's individualism shows up in his almost total neglect of differences among groups. Group differences place far heavier demands on tolerance, however, than do individual differences. The uniqueness of a single individual is apt to be merely surprising or amusing; it is the uniqueness of parties, races, classes, and nations that arouses passion. For someone to develop odd characteristics and habits is not likely to provoke much intolerance on my part, whereas for him to join a political group that I despise may tempt me to forget that he is human.

To emphasize the need for tolerance in relation to social differences, however, risks obscuring the principal truth that concerns us, for to speak of social differences is to speak of uniqueness. The principal truth that concerns us is that the imperative of tolerance derives its authority from the mystery of personality—something that may be manifest in individual or group uniqueness but that also, as in some of the greatest personalities, may not be manifest in any readily describable form at all.

But what is there in mere personal being, apart from individual or social uniqueness, that calls for tolerance? Is not such tolerance as easy and natural as permitting someone to agree with your own opinions? That this seems at first to be so indicates how difficult it is to remain aware of the depths of personal being and not reduce it to something superficial and adventitious, such as uniqueness. To be authentically in the presence of another person is to be outside the kind of everyday, calculable security that is provided by a world of familiar objects. It is also to be humbled, since a person as such is not an object of power. In short, entering into an "I-Thou" relationship entails the loss of both security and personal ascendancy. José Ortega y Gasset has effectively pointed to this truth in stressing the extent to which uncertainty and crisis are inherent in human nature. If such a view seems doubtful, the reason for this may be that the established forms of society are designed to shield us from the fundamental realities of personal being and that most of us are not often truly and deeply in the presence of another human being. Is there not a certain subtle intolerance inherent in every social order—an intolerance that works not so much by suppressing differences as by facilitating superficial relationships? The Athenians found that they could not tolerate Socrates even though, as in the case of Lincoln, the term "representative" was fully as applicable to him as the term "unique."

Thus the ideal of tolerance does not depend on the notion that individuals can be or should be unique. Does it depend on the notion that they can be or should be separate from one another? The ideal of personal separateness, as distinguished from that of uniqueness, must be discussed briefly in its relation to the concept of Tolerance,

Some of Mill's imposing confidence in the desirability of tolerance was due to his belief that much of an individual's life has little influence on the welfare of anyone else. If this belief is rejected, however, it may seem that everything is the business of everyone. How can tolerance then be defended?

The answer can be stated concisely, partly because it restates a point already made; it is an important answer however, if we are to understand the nature of communal, as opposed to individualistic, tolerance. To be sure, veracity and responsibility are not self-regarding; it is of the utmost concern to everyone that as many people as possible realize these qualities. As had already been shown shown, however, these qualities are essentially free; in the nature of things, one is veracious and responsible voluntarily or not at all. The same can be said of community. If it could be forcibly created, surely it should be; but enforced relationships cannot possibly be communal. The idea of tolerance does not depend on the existence of activities that affect no one but their author; what is important is that there be activities that cannot be subjected to compulsion without being destroyed. [8]

Thus, in dealing with the inevitable cohesion, as well as with the fated similarity, of individuals, the concepts of veracity and responsibility help to liberate us from an unrealistic and morally invalid individualism.

The concept of tolerance I am trying to formulate may be brought into view in its entirety by succinctly contrasting it with

Mill's concept of tolerance. The individualistic tolerance of the essay *On Liberty* expresses indifference toward the other (since the individual's supreme aim is his own autonomy and uniqueness), and separation from the other (since the individual can inhabit a sphere in which he is neither very much affected by, nor very much affects, anyone else). Communal tolerance, in contrast, expresses attentiveness. It is a form of waiting for the other. For Mill, to be tolerant was to practice a kind of disengagement; I have tried to argue here that tolerance should be viewed, instead, as a kind of relationship.

These considerations seem to me to justify the conclusion that the new concern for community, and the new realization of the force of conditions making for similarity and cohesion, does not jeopardize the ideal of tolerance. On the contrary, it makes that ideal more humane and thus stronger than it was under liberal auspices.

Certain misunderstandings of community, however, do jeopardize tolerance. Hence it seems appropriate to conclude this section with a brief discussion of two such misunderstandings, both productive of intolerance at the present time. Doing this may help to clarify the viewpoint I am seeking to develop.

5

Let us first consider the idea of what might be called "the righteous society." This idea figures today in the intolerance of both the Right and the Left.

Proponents of the righteous society envision community as collective adherence to an absolute and clearly known moral law. Their main premises, then, are the reality and the knowability of the moral order. The conclusion based on these premises is that men must be disciplined by the law. The rules of righteousness must be set down in a changeless code, and people must be forced to revere and obey those rules. Community is realized through common subjection to the law. The communal attitude entails not waiting for those who can appear only through individual responsibility and veracity, but demanding that eveyone submit to the law. A community member is one who knows how men should behave, who so behaves himself, and who recognizes as fellow members of the community those who behave as he does. In short, the human bond is not tolerance but right.

The most powerful expressions of this ideal are found in the Old Testament. The very reality of Israel, as depicted there, lay in its possession of the law brought down by Moses from the smoking mountain. The concept of the righteous society is not merely ancient history, however; it still has followers. This is evident when conservatives denounce the permissiveness of parents and schools and tell us, in effect, that we long ago discovered what is right and that our duty now is simply to see that it is done. On the other side, the Left evinces its own belief in the righteous society in the bitter certitude with which it condemns the sins of the powerful. Young reformers and revolutionaries often reproduce the anguish and self-righteousness, although not often the grandeur, of the prophets of ancient Israel.

It will be apparent to the reader that this viewpoint is far from contemptible. It is founded on a wise mistrust of man (I will take up the implications of this mistrust, with respect to tolerance, in the third section of this chapter), and there is a kind of moral splendor in its allegiance to the right.

What seems to me erroneous in the concept of the righteous society is the idea, first, that some people know what righteousness is and, second, that they can compel everyone to be righteous. As for the first idea, we should be careful not to assume that we have perfect moral knowledge merely because we feel confident in the validity of certain general rules ("Thou shalt not kill," for example), or because we can recognize with assurance acts that are thoroughly evil (such as Eichmann's organization of the Jewish deportations). Although the validity of certain standards may be incontestable, precisely how they should be applied is most uncertain; a good example of this is the difficulty in applying the prohibition against killing to war. And while it is clear that vast evil is sometimes done, we cannot with any assurance estimate the degree or kind of wickedness present in the participants. [9] Thus, without questioning the reality of absolute values, I suggest that we live in a state of moral doubt. Even if we did not, however—and this brings me to the mistaken idea that we can compel everyone to be righteous—we still could not create a righteous society, because righteousness is essentially voluntary. The notion of performing a virtuous act under compulsion is self-contradictory, and the notion that one will perform a virtuous act because it has been taught since infancy and has become habitual is equally self-contradictory.

In sum, man feels the demand upon him of what absolutely ought to be, but this demand is not translatable into either a system of moral knowledge or a set of social and political relationships. I suggest that the kind of community that is within our reach consists less in the common realization of righteousness than in the common search for it. What ought to be transcends even the best of what actually is, and for this reason righteousness should be thought of as inquiry rather than final accomplishment.

Another misunderstanding of community that deserves brief attention is particularly characteristic of the contemporary Left. It is incorporated in a concept of what might be called "the natural society."

Radical students today often suggest that once the governing few are deprived of their power and privileges and the people possess the wealth deriving from modern technology, joyful associations in work and play will arise spontaneously. Churches will disappear; culture will no longer be created by a few, enjoyed by the privileged, and confined to concert halls and museums. Man will be liberated from the unreal worlds created by established religion and by upper-class culture. Herbert Marcuse expresses the ideal of the natural society when he writes approvingly of "the insistence that a socialist society can and ought to be light, pretty, playful." [10]

The concept of the natural society is at the opposite pole from that of the righteous society. Instead of stern regulation, it proposes complete liberation; instead of discipline, spontaneity.

Superficially, it is more tolerant. Where unity is total and spontaneous, however, tolerance is not needed. Thus the ideal of a society "light, pretty, and playful" does not threaten to produce active intolerance so much as it tends to dissolve the sense of reality and the self-discipline on which tolerance depends. A tolerant man is inured to the failures of understanding that make it necessary for us to tolerate one another; he is self-restrained enough to maintain a posture of attentiveness rather than coerciveness. The Hippie movement exemplifies the effort to live according to the canons of the natural society, and it must be admitted that its participants have on the whole been tolerant. But is their tolerance durable? I fear that it is heavily dependent on sentimentality and youthful good spirits and will pass with these.

The effort to establish community either through the harsh discipline of righteousness or through the abandonment of all discipline is likely to lead to the very opposite of community—to a

violent and mindless unity in which the essential self is totally suppressed. Community depends on a capacity to wait for that which
becomes present only through veracity and responsibility.

Let us turn now to the second great challenge to tolerance—that
of "transrationalism."

TOLERANCE AND TRUTH

To many liberal intellectuals, any kind of transrationalism imperils
tolerance. Such an impression is not baseless. Modern man's confidence in reason and the skill with which he has used it have certainly contributed heavily to the growth of tolerance. Men like the
philosophes in eighteenth-century France resisted the dogmas of
royalty and clergy because they were convinced that an understanding of man and society could be reached by reasoning and that no
reliance should be placed on doctrines developed in any other way.
Their demand that they be allowed to reason freely was in effect
a demand for tolerance. Correspondingly, the intolerance of royalty and Church represented a kind of transrationalism; people were
not allowed to commit themselves wholly to the guidance of reason. At the very least, therefore, it has to be admitted that rationalism and tolerance are often allies.

This is perhaps not only the least, however, but also the most
that can be said. Plato was at the same time highly rationalistic
and highly intolerant (according to the most common, and to my
mind most plausible, interpretation of his works). On the other
hand, transrationalism is by no means uniformly intolerant. Bud-
dhism, for example, is typically less respectful of reason than are
most kinds of Christianity; it is also typically more tolerant than
Christianity. Generally speaking, the Far Eastern religions are mystical and tolerant. Within Christianity, a similar conjunction of
attitudes is apparent in Quakerism, which is transrationalist in its
adherence to the idea of the "inner light" but consistently tolerant
in relation to other faiths.

To settle the question (or to come as near to settling it as this
kind of question permits) requires theoretical analysis; historical
generalizations can bring out factual tendencies but not the logically necessary relationships we are concerned with when we ask
whether transrationalism means intolerance. And what theoretical
analysis requires is a more specific definition of the meaning of

of transrationalism than has so far been offered. Just as the reconciliation of community and tolerance depended on assigning the
term "community" a certain meaning—one at odds with the conceptions of both the left and the right—so the reconciliation of
transrationalism and tolerance depends on laying down some kind
of first principle concerning the nature of understanding. In what
does its transrational character consist?

This brings me to one of the critical points in this essay—the
explanation of a principle that not only does much to undergird
the ideal of tolerance but also interlocks with, and in that way
supports, the concept of community suggested in the preceding
section. It may be termed "the principle of uncertainty."

1

Broadly, I wish to argue that although man cannot, now or ever,
place unreserved confidence in his rational knowledge, he is not
justified in wholly repudiating reason in his search for truth. The
power of reason is limited, but it is real. This means that man must
engage in reasoning but in doing so must expect to reach boundaries beyond which reason alone cannot pass. I think the key to tolerance lies in thus respecting reason but not overestimating it—in
recognizing that it may disclose something of absolute being but
cannot provide final and all-embracing knowledge. The intolerant
are perhaps those completely lacking either in respect for reason
or in reservations concerning it. The principle of uncertainty represents an effort to avoid these two extremes.

In a very general form, the principle goes back to ancient
Greece and is an enduring element in philosophical history. Plato's
philosophy, for example, is a compound of reason and myth; and
in the thought of Thomas Aquinas reason is indispensable for
reaching understanding but needs to be guided, and ultimately replaced, by revelation.

Even in the specific form that I shall suggest for the principle—
one emphasizing, more than is customary in Platonism or Thomism,
the discontinuity of the rational and the suprarational—there is a
transrationalist tradition. For Socrates, who evinced a profound
and balanced understanding of reason, the process of rational argumentation was apparently the source of a kind of holy ignorance—
a state of rational doubt that was the obverse side of an awareness
of ultimate being. It is possible that Socrates' understanding of

reason is given its most adequate philosophical form not in the idealism of Plato but in the dualism of Immanuel Kant. As a philosopher of the Enlightenment, Kant was far from contemptuous of reason; he was a defender of science and of rational morality. Yet, in limiting reason to appearance, he directed attention to areas that could be entered, if at all, only by transrationalist insight. The thinker who probably did more than any other to open up these areas was Søren Kierkegaard. For all of his insistence on faith and his defiance of rationalists like Hegel, however, Kierkegaard remained highly respectful of reason and was himself a careful and indefatigable reasoner. The dual regard for the power and for the limits of reason that is embraced in the principle of uncertainty is expressed in Kierkegaard's assertion that "the paradox is the source of the thinker's passion" and that "the supreme paradox of all thought is the attempt to discover something that thought cannot think." [11]

Finally, the great German thinker of our own time, Karl Jaspers, may be interpreted as a twentieth-century Socratic, with his relation to Socrates mediated by Kant and by Kierkegaard. The following reflections owe a great deal to Jaspers.

Thus what I hope to show is not just that there is a conceivable form of transrationalism that accords with tolerance. Although the principle of uncertainty must be set forth to some extent in my own terms, I hope to show also that a true and balanced appraisal of the powers of reason—one attested to in various ways by a series of great thinkers extending back to ancient Greece—supports the ideal of tolerance. Before outlining the principle of uncertainty, let me endeavor to reduce the vulnerability of my argument by means of two preliminary comments.

First, the principle of uncertainty is not intended as a claim that we possess no assured rational knowledge at all. Presumably, the laws established in many areas of the physical sciences can be characterized as absolute. Moreover, I am willing to grant the possibility, if not the present reality, of authentic psychological and sociological laws; there is no incompatibility between transrationalism, as I conceive it, and the behavioral approach so widespread among academic students of society and politics. And, even beyond the boundaries of science, the principle of uncertainty is not meant to imply that every explanation is equally doubtful. Although there is no demonstrably true world-view, for example, it would be possible to construct a demonstrably false one; this could be done by making it self-contradictory or by setting it in opposition to empirically verifiable facts. I believe that all real knowledge is affected by uncertainty without being destroyed by it, and that, while no world-view is scientifically absolute, we are not thereby plunged into a nighttime of doubt in which the wildest fancies can be seriously entertained.

The second preliminary comment is that I depend on the indulgence of the reader. To be accommodated in an essay devoted to political theory rather than epistemology, my argument must be sketchy. It may seem inadequate also in that it is not the work of a professional philosopher; I will suggest answers to questions to which great philosophers have devoted years. My justification is simply that I do not see how otherwise it is possible to deal philosophically with a problem such as tolerance or indeed with any other political problem. In short, I do not see how political philosophy can avoid these weaknesses.

I have tried to reduce these weaknesses, however, by seeking direction and support at every step in Kant's *Critique of Pure Reason*, especially as interpreted in the writings of Karl Jaspers. Of course one cannot adopt another's philosophy—even one framed by a thinker of the first rank—without introducing variations. One cannot be a philosophical slave, even of Kant's. I am fully responsible, then, for the following reflections. I hope, nevertheless, that my views may draw strength from their Kantian roots.

The basic idea I wish to suggest, the idea from which the principle of uncertainty will be drawn, is simply that our rational knowledge is essentially incomplete. The word "essentially" deserves emphasis. Its use in this context implies that the incompleteness of our rational knowledge is inherent in the nature of such knowledge and cannot be overcome or even affected by further inquiry. This means not that our knowledge cannot be widened indefinitely, but only that certain realities cannot be included within it.

How can the limits of knowledge be identified? The answer, I think, is by reflecting on consciousness. On reflection, it is clear that we are conscious not only *through* knowledge but *beyond* knowledge as well, and that consciousness discloses characteristics of reality that reason is essentially incapable of grasping. In other words, we seem to be *aware* of realities that we cannot altogether *know*. I suggest that there are three of these.

1   *Myself*   Of course I do have some knowledge of myself—
of my age, sex, profession, and so forth. Beyond such knowledge,
however, and regardless of how extensive it may be, I am aware of
aspects of myself that I cannot get outside of and know in the
same way I know the observable, describable self. As we have seen,
one of these aspects is simply the I that, rather than being known,
does the knowing. Knowledge is of objects. For there to be an object, however, there must be a subject; this is true even when I myself am the object. In this way, the essential structure of knowledge
seems to entail the impossibility of man's ever being wholly something known. The nature of the knowing self cannot be described;
if it could it would be known—an object rather than a subject. We
are aware of that unknowable self, however, whenever we know
another reality.

In addition to the knowing self, I am aware of a deciding self. (The
question as to why we are sure that these are one self need not be
considered here.) Whereas objects that are known are determinate, in
the sense that they have definite characteristics, the deciding self is
indeterminate, or free. I know many things, but not what I will do. I
may resolve to act in a certain way, but my knowledge of what I will
do is essentially different from my knowledge, say, of what will happen when I hold a match to the wick of a candle. I am aware that I
do not have to do what I have resolved to do. In other words, I know
the realities around me as a set of possibilities rather than as finished
objects of contemplation, and the counterpart of these possibilities is
my freedom. The non-objective, unknowable character of freedom
comes out in the thought of Hegel and Sartre, where freedom is discussed as a power of negation; from this point of view, if an object
such as a desk *is*, then freedom in a sense is nothing—it is not an object—although its nothingness can be related to the desk, for example,
by destroying it. It is often asserted, of course, that freedom is an illusion, and it is true that when we look at man as an object of research we must assume that each of his acts is causally determined.
The consciousness of freedom, however, remains ineffaceable, for
one cannot regard human beings wholly as objects of research;
sometimes one must *be* a human being and then one is compelled
to make choices and, at least tacitly and temporarily, set aside all
deterministic presuppositions.

Finally, I am aware of myself through feelings that elude the
kind of public definition that would be necessary if the self

disclosed through these feelings were to be an object of rational knowledge. It is not easy to explain this elusiveness. The explanation is not always, and perhaps not ever, that the feelings are unique; this is shown by the fact that they are expressed (but not objectively defined and known) in works of art, such as symphonies and poems. It may lie rather in the way in which they absorb the whole self, so that they are destroyed as soon as one gains the detached and observant standpoint from which they might be studied. For example, the experience of sorrow is very differently related to the self than is the experience of the color blue. It is true that neither experience can be defined in a manner that permits the definition to replace the experience; a person blind from birth cannot experience the color blue through hearing it defined. The difference lies in this: that sorrow pervades one's whole consciousness (one is "filled with sorrow") so that it is impossible to stand off and observe it as one observes a color. In other words, one can *know* sorrow only by *being* sorrowful, whereas no comparable statement can be made about the color blue. This suggests that the ineffable feelings are those that constitute a way of being; hence one experiences them only by losing his scientific detachment and entering into them. If this is so, then no kind of scholarly effort to incorporate all inward feelings in objective knowledge—the kind of effort sometimes made in psychology or phenomenology—can possibly be successful. It will be checked by feelings that are experienced only when they displace the attitude in which one rationally inquires and knows—feelings that, strictly speaking, can be lived but not known.

Awareness of myself is not an intuition of a definable entity. I cannot fit the ideas of subjectivity, freedom, and exclusively inward feelings together to make up a single coherent picture of the self. Those ideas represent ways in which I apprehend the self through what might be called "non-knowing," although that non-knowing is a kind of consciousness.

2 *The other* My rational knowledge is like a circle of light. On one side, light falls on me, although I am partly in darkness; on the other side, light falls on the other person. Moreover, just as in knowing myself I am aware of aspects of the self that are not known, so in knowing the other I am conscious that my knowledge is incomplete—that the other also is partly in darkness.

Less metaphorically, I am conscious in the other of the

subjectivity, the freedom, and the inwardness that I find in myself. Our awareness of these qualities in others is as indubitable as our awareness of them in ourselves, despite the fact that it is not obvious how we gain such awareness. Hence our rational knowledge is incomplete on the side of the object as well as on that of the subject. (This is to refer primarily, of course, to those objects that are human beings. It is not clear, however, that the mystery one senses in persons is an exclusively human characteristic.) To elucidate this lacuna in our knowledge, it is necessary to consider how we come to our consciousness of the subjectivity, freedom, and inward feelings of the other.

It appears to me that each of these rationally unknowable aspects of the other enters my consciousness in a different way.
1.   I become aware of the subjectivity of the other not only in sharing an object, as when together we lift something heavy, but in a more poignant experience: when I become an object for the other. This happens not only if I am physically attacked but even if I am looked at in a certain way. In his great work *Being and Nothingness*, Sartre has discussed at length the power of "the Look." 2.   I am aware of the freedom of the other through not knowing altogether what he will do. Of course I know in part; civilization would be impossible if we could not count on many regularities in human behavior, that derive both from institutions and from human nature. But there is a residue of uncertainty, and in framing our expectations of the future such doubt is not at all negligible. With the development of nuclear weapons, for example, we are deprived of assurance even that the human race will survive. 3.   We attribute feelings to others like those we are conscious of in ourselves because, while our "deepest" feelings cannot be embodied in objective knowledge, they can be communicated. Only great writers do this fully and consistently and often ordinary people find themselves locked up with feelings no one else can comprehend. Nevertheless, through art as well as through acts of communication that are now and then accomplished in every life, the doors of inwardness are opened sufficiently for one to be sure that he is not the only creature with moods and passions that cannot be objectively comprehended.

The unknowability of the third reality that checks the impulse of reason toward completeness is manifest in the fact that all of the usual names for it are inappropriate, since they connote qualities that we could attribute to it only if we could know it. I shall use a term that seems no more unsuitable than any other.

3 *Being as a whole*   The inappropriateness of this term stems from the fact that being is not accessible to us as a whole and we therefore have no right to assume that it is a whole. Some such term seems unavoidable, however, in dealing with the fact that our rational knowledge is inherently incapable of reaching totality. Karl Jaspers has expressed the idea very simply in speaking of "the endlessness of experience," a concept he derived from the antinomies of Kant. We cannot discover the cause of an effect without asking about the cause of that cause; we cannot conceive of a limit in space without conceiving of a space beyond that limit; we cannot think of the simple parts making up a composite whole without thinking of parts presumably making up those parts. Reason presses backward in time, outward in space, and inward in its analysis of matter, but it does not discover any unconditional beginning, any final spatial limit, or any ultimate constituent of matter. And not only is our knowledge in this way empirically inconclusive; we cannot even imagine a first beginning, or a limit in space, or a simple element. Thus we are barred from assuming there are such realities; moreover, we cannot even speak of them, except to characterize the ideal of completeness that reason aims at but can never reach.

Each person, of course, lives within what appears at any particular moment to be "the world"—all-inclusive and rounded out. But this world changes in the course of one's life; and it is quite different for a person in one culture than for someone in another culture. Further, owing to "the endlessness of experience," we cannot make philosophical sense out of the idea that the world is equivalent to being as a whole; we cannot expand our picture of the realities around us into a meaningful picture of all reality. But if we cannot conceive of being as a whole in the way we conceive of the world immediately around us, this means that, in the ordinary sense of the word, we cannot conceive of it all.

My entire argument that rational knowledge is essentially incomplete may be summarized by saying that I myself, others, and being as a whole are not objects. We are so used to dealing with objects that we tend to assume that everything that is real is some kind of an object. An object, however, is a very specific kind of reality; according to common usage, it is a finite entity, with a spatial and temporal location, which I can observe and rationally comprehend. The above reflections suggest that certain realities—and not distant, hypothetical realities, but rather the self and the other, as well as encompassing being—are not objects. Certain aspects of man's behavior can be objectively comprehended, in psychology and sociology, but the self and the other are not wholly included in the knowledge thus gained. Physical reality lends itself to objective comprehension more readily than does man, in that the non-objectifiable aspects of an entity like a rock or a tree are more negligible than the non-objectifiable aspects of a person; nevertheless, we cannot objectify even physical reality in its entirety.

This discussion began with the concept of *uncertainty*; most of it has been taken up, however, with the concept of *incompleteness*. How are these related? It will be clear that from the point of view I am suggesting not everything is uncertain. It seems to me that recognition of what is certain, through being rationally known, and the effort to extend our certainty as far as possible, are no less important than awareness of the limits of certainty. To ignore rational certainties is to be open to every kind of sentimentality and blind belief. If there were no certainties at all, the mind could become willful and self-indulgent and man could become oblivious of his finitude. In this way, the scientific attitude, in the study both of the physical world and of society, is essential to the stance in which man recognizes his limits, lives with discipline, and has care for the truth. Defenders of morality and religion have sometimes looked on science as an enemy that would transform all being into cold, calculable objects. When they do this, however, they weaken the principle that there are limits to the possibilities of life and belief, and this must ultimately be as harmful to morality and religion as to science. Hence the argument that our knowledge is incomplete is not intended to deny or depreciate the certainties that surround us—certainties we rightfully try to reinforce and extend.

Owing to the incompleteness that necessarily characterizes human knowledge, however, uncertainty is a fundamental characteristic of consciousness. Not only is our knowledge limited, so that although we know many things we do not really know comprehensively either ourselves or the universe we inhabit. But in this situation we cannot even determine the significance of what we do know. It is not too much to say, consequently, that rational uncertainty is a primary constituent of our lives.

Although our uncertainty is a single environing condition, and thus a whole rather than a compound of distinct components, it may prove convenient to consider two aspects of this condition. Our uncertainty affects our knowledge of particular entities, such as individual human beings (in Kant's terms, "things-in-themselves"), and also our knowledge of being as a whole. Let us discuss these two aspects in turn.

The preceding analysis indicates that, while we do not and cannot possess knowledge of things as they are in themselves, we can be conscious of them in various ways. Kant seems to say in some passages of the *Critique of Pure Reason* that this is not so and that we can gain no consciousness of things-in-themselves beyond the bare realization that they must exist. But succeeding thinkers have repeatedly found this a difficult doctrine to accept. For one thing, it invites the rejoinder that if the things-in-themselves are totally outside of our consciousness, then they are nothing to us. If this argument is pushed to its limit, the conclusion is not merely that we can forget the things-in-themselves, since our lives are in no way affected by them, but also that we have no right even to attribute reality to them; if we can know nothing about them, we cannot know that they are real. But more basic than any such theoretical consideration is the fact that men are bound to struggle against the confinement Kant imposes on them. Kant places man in a kind of ontological prison, altogether alienated from being, due to the nature of his sensual and intellectual faculties. But not only metaphysical thought from the time of Plato to that of Heidegger, but science as well, evinces a strong desire to get into touch with ultimate realities. This desire is of sufficient force that life in a Kantian universe would be a kind of dreadful dream, with no possible awakening.

It turns out, on more comprehensive examination of Kant's writings, that Kant himself was apparently unwilling to accept the ontological alienation seemingly affirmed in some passages of the first Critique. Thus, for example, in the *Critique of Practical Reason* Kant infers from our consciousness of the moral law that man is free. True, freedom is not a matter of natural knowledge, like the law of gravity. Yet, for Kant, we do know, beyond all possible doubt, at least this one thing about every person as he is in himself: he is free. Examples of this sort are numerous in the critical writings. What they show is that Kant did not adhere to an extreme dualism. There is consciousness, if not knowledge, of things in their primal reality.

Assuming, then, that this is the case, what can we say about our uncertainty so far as it affects our relations with individual entities? The answer can best be put, perhaps, in terms of the inadequacy of our knowledge.

In the first place, the very fact that knowledge of the self and the other is incomplete implies that it is inaccurate; the entirety of my knowledge does not—and cannot—correspond with the entirety of the reality thus known. Further, transrational consciousness of the self and the other (in some instances even when the other is not human) discloses qualities diametrically opposed to those disclosed through knowledge. For example, I am aware of the self as free, whereas all I know rationally is causally determined; every entity I encounter is particular, whereas I know only the general. Finally, scenes of natural beauty, artistic masterpieces, the great philosophies, and the major religious traditions often intimate, or purport to disclose, truths of which knowledge gives no hint—for example, eternity, and the dignity of the individual. In short, our transrational consciousness of individual entities shows us not only that our knowledge of those entities is incomplete but that we have no way of gauging its scope or significance.

This uncertainty has important practical results. Knowledge can help us in dealing with the realities around us, once we have determined how these realities ought to be dealt with; but knowledge does not enable us to make that determination. What is the proper aim of life, immediate happiness or salvation? Is a criminal morally evil or only psychologically ill? Does a beautiful painting disclose the truth about reality or only the artist's fantasies? Every reality can be seen in a variety of ways; our knowledge of a reality does not combine all the possible ways of seeing it but is only one among them. This is particularly manifest in the case of a human being. Consider, for example, someone whose portrait is familiar to many people—the wife of the painter Paul Cézanne. Her awareness of herself, Cézanne's awareness of her, what Cézanne saw when he painted her, what the Catholic Church said about her ultimate destiny, what her physician knew and a psychoanalyst might have discovered, all refer to the same being and yet cannot be brought together as *knowledge* of that being.

The other kind of uncertainty concerns the relationship not of

the empirical object to the thing-in-itself but of the totality of
knowledge to being as a whole. I have said that being as a whole is
not an object; this implies that it is not possible to make any rational judgment concerning its nature or meaning. Suggestions
emerge from art, philosophy, and religion, but none of these is rationally compelling; seldom, indeed, do any of them have any intrinsic rational weight at all. Most religious doctrines, for example,
find little support in rational knowledge, and the problem for theo-
logians is not to prove them but to formulate them so that they
are not subject to disproof. Likewise, every philosophy turns on
some central insight that is not rationally demonstrable. Even posi-
tivism, in its initial resolution not to pass beyond what is scientifically demonstrable, takes a position that is not itself scientifically
demonstrable.

In consequence, man is free to construct a variety of world-
views. Not that he is free to adopt any view that happens to appeal
to him. Empirical knowledge implies some constraints; one cannot,
for example, rationally accept the biblical account of creation as
a literal truth. The rule of logical consistency also delimits the
range of philosophical construction; thus one cannot believe both
that morality is purely natural and that God addressed Moses on
Mount Sinai. But no definite philosophies are implied in this way.
Empirical knowledge does not in its totality constitute a world-
view, although it is meaningless and useless unless it is subordinated to a world-view. Likewise, the rule of logical consistency only
limits the variety of philosophical orientations that one can assume;
it does not prescribe any one of them.

Further, not only *may* man choose among various possible
world-views but he *must* as well—if only by refusing to choose deliberately and thus acquiescing in one of them or in some mixture
of them that has been thoughtlessly absorbed in the past. Suspension of judgment is possible as an intellectual posture but not as a
vital posture—not as an attitude with which one can carry on his
life. For example, one must live as though God is either a reality
or an illusion; one must behave politically according to the maxim
that the aim of the state is freedom or that it is some kind of order; one must assume that men are essentially equal or that some
have unique dignity; and so forth. One may remain ready to change
his mind, but there is no way to avoid at least provisional commitments. The fact that in making such commitments people are often

changeable and inconsistent shows not that choice is avoidable but only that human nature sometimes manifests frivolity or confusion. Nor does the inability of some people to articulate, or even clearly recognize, how they view reality show that choice is avoidable. Man must choose some kind of life and in doing that he chooses its philosophical premises.

Thus all that we know must be fitted into a world-view that, properly speaking, we do not know. And our sense of the significance and the proper uses of our knowledge will be determined by this larger setting. The scientific findings of psychoanalysis, for example, are quite different for a Catholic Thomist, a Marxist, and a New Deal liberal.

In summary, I cannot *know* my own nature or that of any other being I encounter, nor can I *know* how I should live. We know what seems like a great deal; but we do not know the ultimate meaning of, or the ultimate purposes which should be served by, what we know; nor do we know whether there are such meanings or purposes. Hence, even though science is one of the most impressive accomplishments of man, and the widening of scientific knowledge one of the most unchallengeable of his aims, a lucid and candid consciousness must always be pervaded by uncertainty.

This premise is neither skeptical nor irrationalist. One reason it is not skeptical is that, as I have already explained and emphasized, it entails no denial of the reality and importance of knowledge. A second reason why it is not skeptical, however, deserves brief comment: it presupposes that man has a capacity for transrational insight, distinct from knowledge, and transrational assurance, distinct from rational certainty. The whole effort to show the limits of knowledge has been an exercise in transrational insight. Thus, man cannot know the self; yet through subjectivity, freedom, and inwardness he can be assured of the reality of such a self and he can gain some insight into it. Without transrational insight and assurance, we could not reasonably discuss the limits of reason.

The history of philosophy, religion, and morality suggests that such insight and assurance go a good deal beyond mere ascertainment of the limits of knowledge. Again and again, men have felt sure of reality without being able to reduce their assurance to forms that could be in any way rationally validated. Socrates, dying serenely despite his rational "ignorance," exemplifies this possibility for philosophy. The history of philosophy is inconclusive rationally, but in every generation thinkers reach transrational insight and assurance. To be sure, they have usually presented their conclusions as being thoroughly rational; but many must have known, like Socrates, that their doctrines were only outward representations, not necessarily compelling for everyone, of an inner assurance.

The history of religions shows the force of transrational assurance even more clearly. It is often assumed that man has only recently begun to realize that the major elements of religious faith are not supported by reason. But skepticism is an ancient philosophical alternative. To consider only the Christian religion, from the time of Paul Christian leaders have been conscious that reason can lead away from faith; and the long centuries of Christian faith did not, one may safely say, depend in any major way on the illusion that what was believed was pure scientific fact. After all, it is not *knowledge* that has been the basis on which Christians have generally professed to live, but *faith*.

Finally, have not people with moral convictions repeatedly shown that our sense of meaning is not totally dependent on rational demonstration? Kant did not suppose that even a thoroughly rational man could be induced by argumentation to adhere to the moral law, and he could not have been unaware that reason might lead to moral relativism. Yet his writings show a prolonged and unwavering confidence in the unconditional authority of the right. Moral insight and assurance were powerfully evinced by some of Kant's later fellow countrymen who, during the Nazi period, calmly died rather than even silently acquiesce in Hitler's tyranny.

The principle of uncertainty, then, does not imply a denial of the possibility of a measure of rational certainty and, beyond that, of transrational assurance; that is why it is not a skeptical principle. But neither is it irrationalist; let us dwell for a moment on this point.

It seems to me that one of the most deplorable practices in the history of Christianity is that of believing contrary to reason. Such an action displays an unlimited and cosmic willfulness; it involves the determination that being must have a certain character even if reason indicates that it does not. Of course, revelation is claimed as authority for doing this; perhaps that reduces the sheer willfulness of the act. However, the readiness of some men to construe revelation so that it is self-contradictory or in conflict with established knowledge, and then adhere to it, suggests a determination to view things as one wishes.

Through reason, we are able to know not only many things that are but many other things that cannot be, because belief in them is either internally contradictory or in conflict with facts. What reason can bring into man's relations with reality is not all-encompassing knowledge but clarity. It enables us to determine what we do know, what we do not but can know, what we cannot know but can believe, and what we can neither know nor believe. If we cease to care about such distinctions, then little is left but wish and fancy, which must be no less fatal to transrational insight than to scientific research.

What I suggest the principle of uncertainty does lead to, rather than skepticism or irrationalism, is a paradoxical view of valid belief and of truth. The preceding reflections indicate that, to be valid, belief must be accompanied by uncertainty. It is easily seen how this rule applies to interpretations of man and to world-views such as those embodied in religions and philosophies. To accept one of these without realizing that it is rationally possible to adopt a different one is to enter into a false relationship with truth and thus with reality, *even if the view one has adopted happens to be true.* Thus, for example, psychoanalytic research has undoubtedly discovered a good deal of truth concerning man; yet to suppose that the Freudian view of human nature is the complete and inalterable truth, precluding alternative views such as the Marxist or the Christian, would be to transform the truth of psychoanalysis into a species of delusion.

The rule that belief must be accompanied by doubt applies, however, even to the acceptance of scientific conclusions, although here we presumably know rather than believe. In adhering to a truly scientific conclusion, one is not obliged, as with a religion or philosophy, to think that he may be mistaken; the conclusion is scientific only if one can accept it with assurance that he is not mistaken. Yet even scientific knowledge is delusory unless it is held with the realization that it is not all-inclusive and does not enable one to determine its relationship to being itself. Scientific knowledge does not disclose its own ultimate significance or proper uses. In this way science as well as philosophy is affected by uncertainty and is a reliable guide to reality only if in accepting it one simultaneously knows and doubts.

Truth, as well as belief, must be interpreted paradoxically. Just as belief is valid only when accompanied by uncertainty, it may be said that truth is genuine only so long as it is accompanied by questions or by countertruths (that is, by other interpretations of the same reality). Thus the truth may be more fully present in an inconclusive conversation, like some of the early dialogues of Plato, than in any specific conclusion left standing alone; and one can feel an immense truth in Kant's antimonies even though the formal result is merely mutual cancellation of theses and antitheses. Here again, as in the case of belief, we find ourselves thinking first of interpretations of man and of world-views rather than of science. There is a sense, however, in which scientific truth also must be interpreted paradoxically. Scientific truth, of course, precludes the possibility of countertruths. But it does not preclude the possibility of questions bearing on its relationship with transrational being, and on this basis it can be said that even science is true only in a dialogical setting.

The idea that reason approaches the truth by questioning and contradicting itself is, on the surface, much like Hegel's view of reason. Hegel believed that even a "true" proposition was actually only partly true and that, by being fully comprehended, it would lead one to a contradictory proposition embodying the truth it omitted. Thus reason progressed by coming into conflict with itself. The trouble with this theory, as I see it, is its claim that the original truth and the countertruth can always be harmonized in a more comprehensive truth. According to this view, thesis and antithesis—to employ a common terminology—can always be combined in a new synthesis; the synthesis, of course, calls forth a new antithesis; but finally all truths and countertruths are reconciled in the absolute truth—an all-comprehensive synthesis. This, however, is hyperrationalism rather than transrationalism. Hegel assumed that reason can finally reach a state of completeness, with no reality beyond it. For this to happen, however, reality must be of the nature of reason; as Hegel himself wrote, "What is rational is actual and what is actual is rational." [12] Perhaps the most unassailable grounds for disagreeing with Hegel are those occupied by one of Hegel's earliest and greatest critics, Søren Kierkegaard. According to Kierkegaard, the Hegelian philosophy in the final analysis suppresses the disclosures of immediate consciousness—the most significant of those disclosures being that of the self. This, as the reader may recognize, is broadly the view expressed in my argument that rational knowledge is essentially incomplete.

The view here suggested is probably much closer to Socrates' philosophy than to Hegel's. (I say "probably" because Socrates, more than most philosophers, is subject to diverse interpretations; one hesitates even to say that he had a philosophy in the usual sense.) Socrates apparently never tired of discussions that opened up conflicts but rarely led to conclusions. Although he avowed at the end of his life that he had reached no knowledge (except of his own ignorance), from what we know, he both lived happily and died serenely. Seemingly, reason had provided him with no complete and absolute explanations, and yet, by leading him repeatedly to its own limits, as encountered in inconclusive discussions, it had given him understanding. Socrates was ignorant in the sense that he could offer no definitive explanations; he was at the same time wise, in that his ignorance was a form of transrational understanding.

In many passages, Mill points toward this kind of position. He writes, for example, that "even in natural philosophy, there is always some other explanation possible of the same facts," and that "truth, in the great practical concerns of life, is so much a question of the reconciling and combining of opposites, that very few have minds sufficiently capacious and impartial to make the adjustment with an approach to correctness." [13] In both of these statements, and in others as well, he suggests the principle of uncertainty. Probably Mill's tolerant attitude (as distinguished from his formal reasons for adhering to the doctrine of tolerance) owes something to this conception of truth. However, this is one of the frequent instances in which Mill's insights and sympathies range far beyond the boundaries of his explicit philosophical commitments. I think that his general position, as judged not just by the essay *On Liberty* but by his writings as a whole, and in particular by *A System of Logic*, was that of a rationalist who believed in the possibility of a final, comprehensive science of man.

This position, as I have argued, underlay Mill's ideal of tolerance. In this respect, moreover, Mill was a typical liberal. From the time of Locke to the present, liberals have called for freedom of thought and speech because they believed that human affairs thus would be brought into the domain of reason.

What are the consequences for tolerance of modifying such rationalism along the lines sketched above?

2

In response to the challenge of communalism, I argued that the

ideal of community, when properly understood, entails an attentiveness equivalent to tolerance. In response to the challenge of
transrationalism, I shall argue that when the limits of reason
are drawn as suggested in the preceding discussion what is implied
is the necessity of an attitude paralleling attentiveness—an attitude
that may be called "openness." Attentiveness and openness are in
reality inseparable and must constitute a single relationship. The
word "attentiveness," however, denotes this relationship as one
between person and person; the word "openness" denotes the relationship as one between person and truth. The substance of the
following argument is that a due appreciation of the power and
the limits of reason imposes on anyone who seeks the truth an in-
defeasible openness.

The basis of this argument is the idea that doubt itself is an element in the realization of being and in this sense enters into an
understanding of the truth. The whole truth cannot be embodied
in a single doctrine, and truth cannot be appropriated in a mood
of absolute certainty. To believe validly one must doubt what he
believes, and to apprehend the truth one must be aware that some
truth may inhere in doctrines he rejects. I believe, for example,
that the principle of human equality is true, but I would not want
to live in a society where no one was permitted to question that
principle; if the principle of equality were made absolute, it would
be turned into a falsehood, rendering a valid belief in equality difficult or impossible. There are, of course, various types of truth—
some, for example, are subject to objective verification and others
not. Some propositions are true on one level and false on another;
the principle of human equality, for example, although spiritually
true, is empirically false. There must, accordingly, be various types
of appropriate doubt. The point I am suggesting, however, is that
there is no kind of truth to which one can be properly related without entertaining some kind of doubt. The readiness to do this is
what I mean by openness. The immediate objects of openness are
unsettling propositions and doctrines; the ultimate object is being
itself.

Truth lies not in isolated minds but in open relationships. Many
people seem to view truth somewhat as they view private property—as a reality that can be definitely identified, that can be held by
one person, and that naturally retains its character and value. If
there is any validity in the concept of truth I have sketched, however, none of these assumptions is warranted: truth is never finally

formulated except, possibly, in the sciences; it is not possessed by one person but, by its very nature, relates one person to another (to believe that something is true, for example, is to believe that it is true for everyone); and it has to be constantly regained. Unlike property, which seems to be essentially something held by one or a few, with others excluded, and which would be meaningless if it did not thus distinguish people as owners and non-owners, truth tends to deteriorate and to disappear precisely when it is subjected to an exclusive claim.

It will be apparent to the reader that what we are considering, in speaking of open relationships, is tolerance. Openness can be expressed and made effective only through tolerance. Hence it can be said that tolerance is nothing less than the sphere of truth.

It may be objected that some of the greatest discoverers of truth have been isolated or persecuted and thus have been excluded from this sphere. This seems to have been so (although perhaps less commonly than is often supposed); but this would disprove the notion that truth lies in open relationships, and thus in a sphere of relationships constituted by tolerance, only if it could be shown that these discoverers have themselves been closed to others. One who is open to truth is attentive to others, even though he may be ignored or threatened with death. In most circumstances, then, it is less crucial to be tolerated than to be tolerant.

Intolerance is inherently untruthful. It presupposes a claim to truth of such a nature that the claim invalidates itself. Correspondingly, tolerance is inherently truthful. This does not mean, of course, that tolerance in itself is apprehension of all the truth one might desire or be capable of apprehending. But tolerance is more than a way to the truth; as recognition of the nature of truth, and of persons in relation to it, it partakes of the truth.

Seen from this angle, the whole question of the probable results of tolerance becomes less decisive than it is for liberal rationalism. Tolerance cannot be regarded as only a means to an end; one is not tolerant merely as a way of reaching a state in which tolerance is no longer needed. Rather, to be tolerant is to dwell in a relationship to ideas and to persons in which truth is inherent. Granted, it is a relationship in which there are always possibilities for rectification, clarification, and deeper understanding; and, granted also, it does not contain in itself all truth but looks toward the truth. In that sense, it is a means. It is also an end, however, for it is a kind of participation in being and in truth. Thus, while a defender of tolerance hopes that tolerance will lead toward truth, he can acknowledge that in fact it may not without turning away from tolerance. He can admit that the clash of ideas may not impel people in the direction of more careful reasoning and firmer convictions; he can admit that the ebb and flow of truth are mysterious. He still is able to see that tolerance is intrinsically a certain way of becoming related to being and thus of laying hold of the truth, and he still can think that, whatever the dangers and drawbacks of tolerance, intolerance is a departure from the very sphere of being and of truth.

The view I am suggesting might be put in terms of inequality and equality. What it does is to deny that there is any vantage point from which some human beings might pronounce conclusively as to the truth and falsity of the opinions of other human beings—so far as these persuasions are internally consistent and compatible with all available evidence. The qualification should be noted. The principle of uncertainty does not require one seriously to consider any kind of nonsense that hysteria or ambition might suggest; it does not entail openness, say, to Nazi racial doctrine. Within very wide boundaries, however, it bars final determinations of the truth or falsity of personal beliefs. This applies not only to religious and philosophical convictions but to political views as well, for the latter must always trace back in some way to the former. The principle of uncertainty requires even the wisest and most learned to admit that the whole truth is not in their possession and that, even if they were cognizant of more of the truth than anyone else, they would destroy it by claiming it as something complete and exclusively their own.

A follower of Mill's might respond that rationalism also requires openness. It is impossible to establish a priori who can reason fruitfully and who cannot; hence a rationalist must be prepared to enter into the reasoning process with anyone. Let us set aside for a moment the fact that the rationalist anticipates a gradual widening of absolute truth with a corresponding narrowing, and final extinction, of the range of questions with respect to which openness is possible. For the rationalist, tolerance is only an expedient. Thus, long before complete and certain truth is reached, he may decide that leaving the arenas of reason open to all is unproductive of truth; this must happen if he concludes, for example, that human beings for the most part are not very rational. It must happen if he comes to believe that inquiry is more likely to succeed if forcibly centered on certain hypotheses to the exclusion of others. A variety of expediential considerations can serve to actualize the potentialities for intolerance inherent in rationalism. As already noted, not only Mill, with his ideal of free inquiry, was a rationalist; so was Plato, with his ideal of the philosopher-king. And it is noteworthy that Plato did not defend tolerance even as a means for arriving at the truth.

The kind of transrationalism I have outlined does accord important functions to reason, as a source both of scientific knowledge and of clarification beyond the boundaries of science. In this way, assuming that relatively few people are persistently and skillfully rational, it grants an advantage in the search for truth to those few. It leaves them in a far humbler position, however, than rationalists accord them. Their adeptness in reasoning is no warrant for their becoming final arbiters of truth.

It must be noted further that the theory of tolerance being outlined here removes various difficulties discussed in the first chapter in connection with the rationalist case for tolerance.

1   A transrationalist concept of tolerance helps us to understand the possibility of the blend of belief and doubt that seems essential to tolerance but is incomprehensible from a rationalist point of view. For a rationalist, believing and doubting are mutually exclusive. One has no right to believe until he has attained rational certainty, and then he has no reason to doubt. The fact that certainty can never be complete, and doubt never wholly removed, does not, as I see it, affect the matter. Doubt and certainty must be inversely proportional to one another. In the same degree in which one approaches certainty, one abandons doubt.

Only a theory of knowledge that establishes a necessary and enduring connection between knowledge and doubt can show how it is possible to say, not just as a disarming social phrase but as an accurate expression of one's attitude, "This is what I believe, although I realize that I may be mistaken." I have suggested a theory according to which this connection lies in the transcendence of being in relation to every rational form. This idea might be given a more adequate formulation than I have succeeded in giving it, but I do think it contains the key to the problem. What seems essential is to establish grounds for holding that it is legitimate to believe without being rationally certain. These grounds must limit the possible scope of rational certainty while providing possibilities of transrational assurance. So long as being is regarded as fully comprehensible through reason, however, and comprehensible in no other way, belief remains tied to rational assurance, and the paradoxical stance of one who is genuinely convinced of a doctrine that he knows to be doubtful remains indefensible.

2   The connection between force and belief is cut more completely than is possible on rationalist premises. I have admitted that the liberal argument that force cannot bring one into a proper relationship with truth, as that relationship is conceived in rationalist terms, is far from baseless; a despotic central power could not easily instill beliefs that are keenly felt and can be rationally defended by those who hold them. It seems to me, however, that a despotic central power could come nearer to doing that than it could to producing the combination of belief and doubt that, from a transrationalist point of view, is essential to valid belief. Rationalism looks toward the attainment of systematic and comprehensive truth. That force might be used in establishing reasoned acceptance of a doctrine purporting to be such a truth is not inconceivable; as I have already pointed out, Catholic doctrine in the Middle Ages was often received by an act of assent that was elaborately reasoned, and certainly sincere, yet also supported with force. On the other hand, it seems altogether impossible that force should be used for bringing into being the duality of conviction and doubt required for appropriating transrational truth. The crucial defect in the intellectual state of Russian Communists today, for example, is not that they lack reasons for being Communists, nor that they are unable convincingly to marshall those reasons, nor, finally, that their beliefs are on the whole demonstrably in error; it is rather that their beliefs are not accompanied (unless secretly and fearfully) by the defined and enduring misgivings that constitute acknowledgement that the whole truth does not lie in any doctrine.

3   The kind of tolerance outlined here is not subject to the difficulty of which Mill himself was so conscious in his own theory of tolerance: that as truth becomes known, tolerance becomes increasingly gratuitous. This difficulty arises in part from the incompatibility, on rationalist premises, of belief and doubt; as man advances toward the truth, doubt is defeated and tolerance left behind. The difficulty also arises in part from viewing tolerance as a

means alone; the attainment of the end renders it unnecessary. If doubt is a necessary element in belief, however, and if tolerance is not merely a means but enters into the end, then tolerance cannot gradually do away with its own justification. We are led, I suggest, to a point of view that both Locke and Mill apparently sensed but never adequately embodied in their arguments for tolerance: that tolerance is not merely an expedient, that it is not merely forced on us by doubts of a kind which should in time be overcome, but is a permanently valid standard of human relations.

In none of these arguments do I mean to deny that reason is important in the search for truth. My intention, rather, is to suggest that the relationship between reason and truth is more complex and paradoxical than is acknowledged in the kind of rationalism represented by Mill. Thus those gifted in reasoning may frequently be leaders in the search for truth; but never can they close the books and declare the search to be finished.

It may help in communicating the idea I have in mind if I rephrase the argument completely, putting it in terms that will serve to show how it differs from the most popular current defense of tolerance, that derived from relativism.

3

The relativistic argument for tolerance is basically simple. All so-called truths, moral principles, and institutions, it is held, can be wholly accounted for in terms of the needs of particular persons and societies; no reference to universal and unchanging moral principles is required. Hence, one can never claim objective validity for his beliefs and practices. This being the case, one is never justified in using force to induce others to share them.

In certain ways, the argument I have been outlining is similar to the relativistic argument. If it is restated in terms of the requirements man places upon man—the normative demands of philosophy, religion, and society—it may be summarized in the proposition that there are no human absolutes. This is to say that no such requirements are unqualifiedly valid and that no systematized combination of them shows man completely and truly what he should be. No moral rules can be followed in every circumstance whatever; to adhere invariably to the rule "Thou shalt not kill," for example, would be to leave the world to criminals and tyrants. Aside from the compromises forced by circumstances, no moral philosophy can scientifically establish the human essence. What is true of the formulations of philosophers and social scientists applies also to the institutions that arise in history. None is perfect or even nearly perfect; and in no society can man realize all of his potentialities.

In other words, man can never get himself fixed in any objective form. He ceaselessly tries to do so, in order to escape the harrowing insecurity of being nothing definite or final. Thus most philosophies purport, however discreetly, to show beyond all serious doubt what man ought to be. Many societies and organizations have claimed to unite man with his essence. For example, one supposedly gains fulfillment by following "the American way of life"; in institutions like the Catholic Church and the Communist Party (although not as these are envisioned by every member), the claim to absolute validity is quite explicit. But man repeatedly finds that something is left out of these forms in which he would so gladly let his human fluidity and freedom congeal; and he feels that what is left out is not something negligible: it is he himself. Everything that man makes, his moral philosophies as well as his tools, his institutions as well as his buildings, serves some needs and not others, can be commended from one perspective and condemned from another, is subject to criticism and change—in short, is relative rather than absolute.

It is apparent how transrationalism leads to an outlook of this kind. There are no human absolutes because man and being are not wholly comprehensible. Realization of this has led thinkers like Edmund Burke to hold that we should rely on custom and tradition rather than on theory. It is hard to see, however, that old societies necessarily embody a fuller and more exact comprehension of man than do philosophies. Some, then, would trust neither in theories nor in institutions but in inspiration—that of great men, as with Carlyle, or of common men, as with Rousseau. But whose inspiration, in its public expression and institutional embodiment, or even intrinsically, contains the whole truth? No theoretical or institutional order is adequate because man and being are essentially transcendent, that is, non-objective, non-abstract, and non-determined.

It may be noted parenthetically that historical pessimism also offers grounds for thinking there are no human absolutes: men are not wise and unselfish enough even to form theories and institutions as adequate as the nature of things allows. This applies particularly to institutions. Institutions are not as malleable as ideas; also, a society cannot operate and endure without inequality and concentrated power, which encourage arrogance and callousness. As a result, societies are invariably more constrictive and oppressive than is necessitated by the bare requirements of order.

The persisting imperfection of human works is perhaps most sharply demonstrated in the fine arts. The arts arise from circumstances in which there is absolute mastery of the materials, so that necessity is wholly subordinated to vision; and presumably artists, unlike politicians, are not morally corrupted by the power they have over their materials. Yet failures are numerous and serious enough to occasion voluminous criticism; and I assume it can safely be said that there are no perfect works of art. If no human absolutes are produced in the fine arts, how much less are they to be anticipated in politics, where the material to be molded is far less controllable and where the temptations to selfishness and superficiality are far greater.

It must be remembered that we are concerned here with standards of morality. I do not think it can be said that there are no absolute truths of any kind. The physical sciences presumably contain some, and there are absolute truths about man as well (for example, man is finite). The truths of the physical sciences, however, have little if any scientifically demonstrable bearing on moral questions; they are not, even implicitly, prescriptive. Hence they do not constitute human absolutes in the sense defined above. As for the absolute truths about man, as argued earlier, even considered as a totality they are incomplete and thus affected by uncertainty. We have some absolute knowledge of man, and may gain more, but such knowledge neither does nor can comprehend a totality of human possibilities. It does not enable one to answer definitively the question, What should I be?

Is not the idea that there are no human absolutes, then, expressive of relativism? Not necessarily. Perhaps, even though every institution and doctrine is relative, there is an unconditional good. If so, then while man should look toward the world of social forms and moral codes with the kind of doubt and detachment encouraged by relativism, he should also look beyond that world with the awe expressed in moral absolutism.

The arguments set forth in this essay roughly suggest a view of this kind—a view holding that there are absolute values but that these cannot be translated into definitive moral philosophies or standards of behavior. One absolute value, presumably, is community. The genuine unity of human beings is good in all circumstances; it need not produce any further good in order to be justified. Yet no actual group is a pure community. Some groups are more communal than others, but all are imperfect. The ancient city-states, for example, have inspired many succeeding centuries with the vision of spontaneous yet civilized communion; but in actuality they were only relatively communal—more communal than Alexander's empire, for example, but in more ways than one productive of alienation.

This is not relativism, in the usual sense. What I am suggesting, so to speak, is not the relativity of all *values* but the relativity of all *evaluations*. Not the good in itself, but historical man—the lawmaker and the philosopher—is relativized.

In contrast with typical absolutism, the good is held to be inaccessible in any objective form. It is impossible in the nature of things for an institution or a doctrine to embody the good adequately. To assert the relativity of all evaluations is to take issue, for example, with the traditional doctrine of natural law (at present certainly the major form of absolutist moral theory). Although the reality of the good can be affirmed, according to the view I am suggesting, its demands on man cannot be rationally and conclusively formulated.

However, it is important to note that, while the relative and the absolute are thus distinguished, it does not follow that they are totally separated. I suggest that the relative manifests the force not only of time and place but also of the unconditional good. It does not do this in a way that makes it possible to distinguish with precision between the relative and unconditional elements in any historical situation; we cannot, for example, say that slavery in Periclean Athens reflects nothing but the historical limits separating ancient man from the good itself, whereas the conversations of Socrates represent the good divested of all historical qualifications. The very idea of doing anything of this sort implies the possibility of defining and objectifying the absolute, or at least its demands on man, thus overcoming relativity. One cannot abstract an institution, or a moment of historical time, and say, "Here the good was fully manifest." One can, however, looking at the historical world through shifting circumstances and insuperable doubts, catch glimpses of something that calls for unconditional allegiance. The authority of these glimpses is not lessened by our inability to say exactly what they are glimpses of.

One of the principal differences between the view I am suggesting, and ordinary relativism, is that moral distinctions among institutions are not barred. For example, one can say that the English political system is better than the Soviet political system; it manifests a more realistic and effective respect for community. The English system is not a human absolute but it is morally superior to the Soviet system.

To rank two or more institutions in order of moral excellence makes it clear that an imperfect institution can in some sense reflect the good. The concept of the better implies the concept, although not the reality, of the perfect. But, apart from all comparisons, many institutions can be seen as in some measure serving humane ends; on the strength of that service, moreover, they can be seen as symbols of community. Universal suffrage might be cited as an example. In the light of unsentimental, empirical analysis, it is drastically inadequate. In America, most potential voters either are politically irresponsible and do not vote at all, or else they vote so habitually for one party that voting, for them, is not a rational act; on the other side, selfish interests usually have little difficulty in shielding themselves from attention and interference on the part of the populace. It hardly needs to be said, however, that universal suffrage contributes something to the cause of justice, although not nearly as much as early supporters hoped that it would. And it is not absurd to see in an arrangement giving one vote to every adult person, regardless of wealth or social standing or any other outward distinction, and vesting ultimate power in the populace as a whole, a symbol of an ultimate communal harmony that cannot be realized by any set of institutions and cannot even be exactly described. Do not many social and political arrangements, such as parliaments, constitutions, and civil rights, contain such symbolic value? So far as they do, a political attitude quite different from either conservatism or radicalism suggests itself—an attitude embodying respect for established institutions without sentimental illusions, and critical insight without hatred.

The lack of human absolutes, then, does not mean that man is adrift, without moral charts, on a sunless and starless sea. One can try persistently to meet the demands of the unconditional (of community), even though no rules or institutions adequately embody those demands. The unconditional will not be found engraved either in institutional structures or in any criticisms or counterprinciples set over against those structures; it will be found, rather, in the realization that both terms in a dialectic of that kind are merely relative. This realization places one in a communal posture—aware of a truth which is intimated but never fully grasped in the course of historical conflict and which demands to be sought in inquiring communication.

Tolerance frees one for such communication. It establishes social circumstances in which the simultaneously critical and respectful historical existence that leads toward the transhistorical is possible. That existence must be dialogical, in spirit, if not in reality—an existence in which man makes decisions, and relates himself to historical realities, yet always in the paradoxical consciousness that his decisions may be wrong and are therefore open to discussion.

Typical relativism simply denies the absolute value of institutions and moral codes. In doing this, it provides no support for tolerance. If there is no absolute good, or if there is such a good but it is unrelated to historical realities, then the gates are open to a nihilism that drowns tolerance in fury or to a historical detachment that nullifies tolerance with indifference. Tolerance cannot resist because every institution designed to protect it, and every proposition ascribing value to it, is radically devalued. Tolerance itself is relativized.

The outlook I suggest precludes both nihilism and historical indifference by affirming the good and its presence in history. But it envisions doubt as an essential element in one's relationship with the good, thus avoiding the risk of a tyrannical absolute. One must enter into history but without binding oneself absolutely to any historical reality. One must divest oneself of both indifference and fury.

Can tolerance be defended otherwise than along some such lines as these? Absolutism makes it difficult to avoid the implication that the good ought to be forced on everyone; relativism can also open the way to force, however, by depriving tolerance of any claim to absolute validity. Perhaps being is such that man can become related to it only by refusing, on the one hand, to affirm unconditionally the validity of his social, epistemological, and moral structures or, on the other hand, to degrade those structures to the level of mere opinion. And perhaps tolerance can be justified only if that necessity is recognized. In other words, if man is to be tolerant, what is perhaps essential is that he be bound by his institutions and beliefs, but not bound absolutely.

I have thus far dealt with two elements of contemporary man's understanding of himself—communalism and transrationalism. Before turning to the third and last, historical pessimism, it seems appropriate to bring out something heretofore only briefly alluded to, that is, the co-ordinate character of the arguments of the first two sections.

4

The idea that the other must be awaited, in his veracity and responsibility, becomes fully comprehensible only in connection with the principle that he is not merely an object of knowledge. He cannot be treated like a set of materials that can be deliberately made into a certain predesigned product. A person is not known only through the study of man—that is at best a beginning; to be known, he must be given the opportunity of being veraciously and responsibly himself. To enter into community requires tolerance because man is not known, or even in principle knowable, prior to the act of communication.

The idea of community, then, can be expressed in terms of uncertainty. When I am uncertain, I make room for the other. I acknowledge that someone else may have understanding that I lack. When I am uncertain, other persons have to be encountered rather than apprehended as objects within a system of knowledge, and to encounter them I can only rest hope in their veracity and responsibility.

If I am absolutely certain, however, I force the other person into one of two positions, either of which precludes communication. If he shares my own total and absolute knowledge, then so far as community is concerned he is identical with me; there is no occasion for communication because we both possess the same definitive knowledge. Thus Plato, in a long and detailed work centering on the recommendation that philosophers should rule, neglects to analyze systematically relations among the ruling philosophers. The reason seems clear: the philosophers possess absolute knowledge and are thus substantially one person. On the other hand— assuming still that I possess knowledge without incompleteness or uncertainty—if the other person is not a subject who merges with me by possessing the same total knowledge I possess, then he is an object that is totally known. Again, there is no occasion for communication. If he is young and has exceptional intellectual powers, he may, like Plato's apprentice philosophers, be gradually drawn up through education to the level of absolute knowledge; but the process of education must be carried on through deliberate control rather than through communication, for the teachers have absolutely nothing to learn. If he cannot become one who knows, then he must remain one who is known, to be observed, ignored, used (possibly for his own good), or even disposed of, as Plato would have disposed of malformed infants.

Proceeding along the same lines, the principle of uncertainty suggests a way of understanding the nature of community. In the preceding section, I proposed that community be envisioned as a common search for righteousness rather than, in the fashion of the Old Testament and of some modern conservatives and radicals, as a realization of righteousness. The linking of community and uncertainty suggests an allied hypothesis: community is the common search for understanding, not the possession of understanding. The idea that community is a sharing of dogma—of doctrines held without uncertainty—is as common as the idea that community is realized righteousness. Calvin's Geneva is a familiar example of a society which assumed that the truth is fully known and that human unity comes from unreservedly accepting it. In our own time, the Soviet Union has, during most of its history, sought unity through dogma. If community presupposes uncertainty, however, the idea of dogmatic community is a contradiction in terms. Community must be, rather, a sharing of uncertainty—an uncertainty which, being shared, is not the frivolous and despairing uncertainty often nurtured by capitalist commerce and democratic politics but a serious and hopeful uncertainty.

In conclusion, transrationalism and community are interlocking relationships with being. Transrationalism means that the notion of comprehending all being is set aside and thus the possibility of communication is established. Community, as here defined, is a search for being in the space between persons rather than in the mind of a single person. Transrationalism prescribes openness, and communalism attentiveness. These two approaches, one an avenue to truth and the other to persons, constitute the tolerance I am trying to describe.

It is not apparent, however, that a communal and inquiring

tolerance is any more likely than the individualistic and rationalistic tolerance of the liberal tradition to bring concrete historical
benefits. In this way it is open to some of the same objections I
brought against the traditional arguments—those summarized under the heading of "historical pessimism." This brings us to the
task of responding to the third and last of the challenges to tolerance discussed in Chapter One.

TOLERANCE AND EVIL

1

Let us briefly recall the issue. According to the sixth traditional
argument considered above, tolerance encourages order (Locke)
and progress (Mill). Thus it is good because it is historically useful.
This argument rested on two assumptions: that man is spontaneously co-operative and that there are natural forces, like the "laws
of supply and demand," that tend to produce harmony and progress even out of competitive and selfish behavior. One element in
the deepened understanding of recent times, however, is a redis-
covery of evil. For many conservatives, order is so fragile and progress so difficult that it is more sensible to concentrate on preserv-
ing civilization than on improving it. Consequently, tolerance is
dangerous. For radicals, typically, mankind is approaching an era
of harmony and peace, but not through the steady diminution of
evil. There is, rather, a final intensification of evil, through class
conflict and war, that in typical radical visions leads at last to harmony and peace. At present evil is dominant; it controls practically
every supposedly humane institution. The main thing our so-called
civilization does for mankind is, as Rousseau said, to "fling garlands
of flowers over the chains which weigh them down." [14] Tolerance is
freedom for oppressors. If conservatives mistrust tolerance because
it threatens established institutions, radicals mistrust it because it
does not. Both of them fear its misuse by iniquitous humans.

What we are dealing with, then, is an increasing sensitivity to
evil. This sensitivity assumes a variety of forms—sometimes that of
an extreme ideology such as conservatism or radicalism, sometimes
that of withdrawal from politics. It ranges from the provisional
pessimism of radicals who think that the evil imposed on us by the
past is on the point of collapsing to the theological pessimism of
Reinhold Niebuhr, who seeks to use the Christian concept of original sin as the basis for a resolute liberalism.

The present discussion does not require us to choose among all such alternatives. One kind of pessimism, however, must be avoided—that in which man is seen as wholly depraved. If no constructive impulses and powers whatever were present in man, then human life would be altogether hopeless; there could not even be tragedy, for there would not be anything great to be destroyed. Extreme pessimism may be summarily rejected by noting that if we were wholly depraved we would neither know nor deplore it. Niebuhr criticizes modern man for his "easy conscience." [15] But the *uneasy* conscience of writers such as Niebuhr is to the credit of man; it shows that he retains at least a consciousness and love of goodness. Thus let us assume only that man is not consistently co-operative and that there are no natural forces that can be relied upon to elicit public benefits from egoistic actions. Let us assume, contrary to the presuppositions of the traditional arguments for tolerance, that man has disorderly and regressive tendencies of appreciable, but not always overwhelming, strength.

This hypothesis represents an effort to come to terms with the impression man has made through his actions in the twentieth century—an impression not wholly bad but nevertheless disturbing. In the West, man has gone much further than ever before in history toward providing a comfortable and civilized life for everyone. At the same time, he has seemed ominously indifferent to the pervasive alienation and the residual injustices that gravely mar, and in the eyes of some morally invalidate, this achievement. In addition, along with his spectacular constructive inclinations and powers, he has shown, through his wars and his death camps, that he has the capacity, and in some circumstances the will, to annihilate everything he has built. We cannot help but entertain disquieting thoughts on human nature. Even though man is not wholly evil, he is, not only figuratively, but in a grimly literal sense as well, an explosive creature. Further, twentieth-century history undermines not only the traditional trust in man but also the traditional trust in the natural forces that were once believed to render even selfish actions orderly and progressive in their ultimate consequences. Extravagantly evil plans, the most lurid example being the design for exterminating all European Jews, have not only been conceived but have been largely fulfilled.

Can tolerance, then, be justified? Given assumptions like those of Locke and Mill, no doubt it can; tolerance is logically seen as opening the way to actions that are, purposely or otherwise, beneficial. If those assumptions are rejected, however, it is easy to conclude that order and progress depend on force and dogma. Tolerance must often turn out to be tolerance of evil. Must it not, then, be condemned?

I think that the kind of tolerance Locke and Mill defended has indeed been largely refuted by the events of the twentieth century. The spirit of their tolerance, and of the tolerance of most liberals, might be summed up in two terms: "utilitarian" and "confident." Their tolerance was utilitarian in that it was intended to serve certain purposes, such as securing order and furthering progress; in this sense it was a form of action. The term "confidence" characterizes their attitude with respect to the efficacy of tolerance and therefore the historical future. In a word, the traditional idea of tolerance is strongly colored by a liberal belief in human initiative and historical progress.

I suggest that tolerance can be reconciled with historical pessimism, but only by abandoning the activism and progressivism of traditional liberalism and adopting a different posture in relation to history. In place of the utilitarian confidence of traditional liberals, I propose what might for the sake of convenience be called "receptive realism." Each of these terms needs to be explained, and I shall begin with "receptive."

Receptivity has been touched on frequently in preceding discussions, since it enters significantly into communal and transrational tolerance, but so far in this essay it has not been given a name. What is receptivity? Negatively, it is abstinence from action based on the realization that the good is given and not produced; positively, it is a readiness for relationships. I have emphasized that community and truth are not deliberate acquisitions but impose a period of waiting; in other words, they have to be received rather than seized. The concept of receptivity is a way of summarizing the orientation of self common to attentiveness and openness. Attentiveness is receptivity in relation to other persons, openness in relation to truth. The usefulness of the concept is that, aside from focusing upon the attitude that is common to attentiveness and openness and thus basic to tolerance, it brings out sharply the difference between the kind of tolerance being sketched in this essay and traditional tolerance.

A receptive tolerance is related to the future through an attitude that can be termed "hope" more accurately than "confidence."

Through receptivity, one directs the self toward possibilities, but one does this with awareness that what is merely possible is not assured. If utilitarian tolerance is a form of action, then receptive tolerance is deliberate inaction. This does not mean a refusal to do anything whatever; as the final chapter will try to show, tolerance does not imply a social policy of mere passivity. Rather, receptive tolerance is inactive in the sense called for in the *Bhagavad-Gita*: one acts in a spirit of inaction, detached from the results. Such detachment stems from the recognition that there is no reliable connection between action and results. To put this in terms that contemporary experience renders comprehensible to almost everyone: in seeking relations with others one cannot be certain of finding them, and the quest for truth may lead into confusion. I am not even sure that community and truth are not sometimes found, paradoxically, by those who have *not* sought them. But to care about these values, while realizing that they are not under human control, is, so long as despair is avoided, to be receptive and hopeful. Utilitarian tolerance is a way of taking the future in hand, whereas a receptive tolerance is a way of leaving the future alone without being unconcerned with it.

Receptive and utilitarian tolerance differ in another way as well. So far as traditional liberalism is utilitarian, it reduces tolerance to a means, and in doing this it deprives it of all intrinsic value. So far as receptive tolerance looks toward the future, it has a like effect. But it contains an element of unconditionality. I suggested above that intolerance is inherently untruthful, and that realizing the truth depends on realizing the incompleteness and hence the uncertainty of one's truth. One can infer that there is truth in tolerance. For like reasons, there is community in tolerance: one is attentive with the hope that a relationship will thus come into being, but the attentiveness is in itself a tenuous relationship. It follows that tolerance is not merely a means to other values; it is a value in itself. From the utilitarian standpoint, tolerance is purely conditional. A receptive tolerance, however, aside from its results, is a partial realization of the ends toward which it is directed.

In summary, receptivity depends not on a calculation of consequences, but on hope and on being in itself a partial realization of the community and truth in relation to which it may also be a means.

Receptivity seems to accord better with the scale of human

failure that we have seen in our time than does the utilitarian activism of traditional liberals. Related to the epistemological principle of uncertainty is the historical principle that man cannot foresee all of the consequences of his actions. This principle is written in our environment—in the ugliness, filth, and poison we suddenly have found all around us—as well as in the indescribable hatred and disorder that have overwhelmed mankind just about when our Victorian predecessors thought we would be reaching the summits of progress. If it is in principle impossible to foresee comprehensively the consequences of our actions, then we are really not entitled to adopt the masterful posture habitual among liberals.

But how is it possible even to be receptive, in view of the power of evil that recent history has disclosed? There are two answers to this question. The first is implicit in the principle of uncertainty: we do not *know* that man is evil. The optimism of preceding generations has been overturned, but nothing definitive about man has been established or can be established. Hence, for us to conclude now that tolerance is bound to lead to disorder and confusion would be just as high-handed a denial of the mystery of being as it was for Locke and Mill to conclude that tolerance would assuredly bring order and progress. It seems to me that Christians have sometimes indulged in this form of human foreclosure. They have inferred from the doctrine of original sin, regardless of both historical experience and the limits of our knowledge, that men need stern and autocratic government. What I have suggested, however, both here and in the preceding chapter, is merely that man is unreliable. If this is so, he cannot be depended on to be always evil any more than he can be expected to be always good. Liberal optimism is objectionable not because it is never justified but because, aside from the fact that it is not always justified, it is an a priori determination. Human beings must undoubtedly be subjected to a number of restraints, but it seems to me that it cannot be decided in advance just where and how these restraints are to be imposed without claiming, at least implicitly, a knowledge we do not and cannot possess.

The second answer to the question as to how receptivity can be justified in view of the apparent power of evil is that it must be linked with the realism referred to above. This brings us to the second term of the "receptive realism" that it seems to me must replace the "utilitarian confidence" of traditional liberals if tolerance is to be reconciled with historical pessimism.

The word "realism" indicates that a receptive society is not necessarily a pure example of vulnerability and naïveté. I would like to think of a receptive tolerance as (in William James's phrase) "tough-minded"—aware of the dangers it may bring on itself and prepared for them. The attitude of realism can be expressed in three propositions.

1   *The risks of tolerance can be reduced through politics.* Tolerance is undoubtedly dangerous in some circumstances. Ancient Athens perhaps would not have lost the Peloponnesian War had it not been for the tolerance that allowed demagogues to arouse inordinate ambitions in the minds of the people. Repression of reckless counsel, however, is not the only way of responding to danger; an alternative is to try to persuade people with prudent counsel. If Pericles had not died early in the war, Athens, while remaining free, might have avoided the actions that led to a Spartan victory. Where freedom is creatively used, a strong political center is probably required. This is suggested not only by Athens, guided in some of its most brilliant years by Pericles and a traditional aristocracy, but also by the only other instance in which freedom gave rise to such cultural splendor, that of Renaissance Florence, where the Medici princes helped to organize the violent energies of individuals.

The tolerance of Locke and Mill was not merely dissociated from politics; it was, as they envisioned it, a substitute for politics in that it released forces making for order and progress, thus rendering the art of deliberately contriving order and furthering progress—that is, politics—superfluous. In this way they left tolerance heavily dependent on their optimistic premises. This implies that those premises may be rejected without jeopardizing the ideal of tolerance, provided political premises—principles concerning the possibility and legitimacy of political art—are put in their place. One of the citizens of Florence at the time of the Renaissance was Niccolo Machiavelli, who achieved a place in the history of thought through his uncompromising and crystalline comments on the art of politics. If there are any large principles implicit in Machiavelli's writings, one of them is this: that order is dependent on politics. If Locke is taken as a symbol of the idea that order is spontaneous, and thus dependent only on freedom, it may be said that the philosophy of tolerance needs to become less Lockean and more Machiavellian.

The politics of a tolerant society, however, need not be concerned only with meeting immediate threats to order. It should be concerned also with creating conditions favoring tolerance and the communication that is the ultimate end of tolerance. In this way, tolerance becomes not only an occasion for politics but also a standard. This subject will be discussed at some length in the final chapter of this essay.

2   *If man is unreliable, then intolerance, as well as tolerance, is dangerous.* Through tolerance, many are set free to do evil; through intolerance, a few are set free, and they may induce many to follow them. One of the persistent oversimplifications in the history of opinion is that repression, while perhaps inglorious, is safer than freedom. This notion arises from the assumption that agents of repression have a selfish interest in order and possibly even in progress. The Nazi regime demonstrated the dubiousness of this assumption. Historical pessimism does imply that one should be apprehensive about tolerance; but it implies that one should be apprehensive about all of man's activities, including that of telling others what they may think and say.

3   *A perfect society is probably unattainable.* Tolerance is unappealing to perfectionists because it promises, at best, a somewhat disorderly and uncertain state of affairs. Many passages in Plato exemplify the distaste for tolerance felt by a man who apparently dreamt of a commonwealth as harmonious and finished as the the Parthenon. He complains of democracies that "the very dogs behave as if the proverb 'like mistress, like maid' applied to them; and the horses and donkeys catch the habit of walking down the street with all the dignity of freemen, running into anyone they meet who does not get out of their way. The whole place is simply bursting with the spirit of liberty." [16] If a fully harmonious society is recognized to be impossible, however, tolerance may seem less objectionable than it did to Plato. The imperfections of a tolerant society may be viewed as inherent in historical existence rather than resulting merely from tolerance.

Realism, in short, is an attitude that is political, attuned to the dangers of total power, and skeptical of perfectionist plans. It depends on a capacity for bearing, without despair, some uncertainty and some evil. In this respect, it may be contrasted with the attitude of those for whom all evil is outrageous and insupportable. Uncompromising hostility to evil is, of course, not the worst of human attitudes. It is morally serious and may be historically

beneficial. Its moral worth should not be taken for granted, however; it often manifests self-righteousness and also a certain weakness—the weakness implicit in being unable to put up with imperfection. Such an attitude has often been manifest among radical
students. It is a primary source of intolerance.

Someone who cannot bear uncertainty and imperfection can be
tolerant only through being very optimistic; in that way evil does
not seem to be of threatening proportions. Perfectionism mixed
with pessimism, however, creates a violent desire to exterminate
the selfishness and unreliability that stand in the way of harmony.
The result admittedly may be a reduction of injustice; but it also
may be the opposite. In any case, it is incompatible with tolerance.
We cannot both be tolerant and aspire to transfigure man.

In summary, I am suggesting that historical pessimism does not
subvert tolerance but calls for a different kind of tolerance than
has been customary among liberals. As receptive, rather than utilitarian, it is an orientation toward possibilities; as realistic, rather
than confident, it is a willingness to suffer the non-fulfillment of
these possibilities.

This kind of attitude is not repugnant to conservatives because
it can be interpreted as a willingness to let things remain as they
are. For the same reason, however, it is offensive to radicals. Receptive realism would strike many of them as a euphemism for
complacency; "bearing some uncertainty and some evil" would
seem to them equivalent to not worrying unduly about injustices
suffered by others.

Suspicions of this kind are not groundless. My argument does
imply that tolerance accompanied by historical pessimism entails
a certain acquiescence in injustice. Further, while I do not think
this necessarily means irresponsibility or inhumanity, having argued the unreliability of men I cannot deny that tolerance is likely
to be used as a facade for self-interested conservatism. Thus I have
no answer to the radical suspicion of tolerance beyond reiterating
what I have already argued: that tolerance is necessary despite its
dangers. However, because the radical criticism is weighty, I think it
is worth restating my argument as it applies to the radical position.

2

Let us begin with the concept of receptivity. In the most widespread forms of contemporary radicalism, receptivity is definitely

precluded. To be sure, it is typically held that the evil in man will wholly disappear sometime in the future and that even now this disappearance is foreshadowed in a few leaders (such as those of China or of Cuba); presumably, a time will come when receptivity is appropriate. Until the moment of human transformation has arrived, however, one must regard most human beings with the utmost cynicism. It is not worthwhile to try to enter into communication with the generality of men because their words, acts, and institutions are selfish and deceitful. This statement may be applied even to the group that is held by most radical visionaries to be the main source of the new society—the working class—for even that group furthers the interests of mankind only through furthering its own selfish interests. Man is so much the creature of economic circumstances that, for the time being, ideals of community and truth are mere sentimentality and a constructive politics must depend on deception and violence. The depth and limits of such cynicism vary among radical movements and thinkers but are found in some degree in most of them.

It is impossible to doubt that a sincere, and sometimes really heroic, desire to liberate men often lies behind this attitude. At the same time, it seems to me, it reifies man as definitely as does the capitalist ideology it attacks. It does this by subordinating him wholly to economic conditions, thus refusing to accept him as a participant in the search for righteousness and truth. The sublimity of the final hope associated with this attitude does not nullify its dehumanizing impact. This impact can be seen in the terror and bureaucratization that have arisen in connection with some of the most determined efforts to achieve justice.

Receptivity means acknowledging the mystery of others and granting them space. The results of doing this are often, if not usually, disappointing. I submit, however, that the results of not doing it—at least the results for personality and community—are likely to be worse. The refusal of receptivity signifies either indifference toward others or else an interest that is purely manipulative, an unconditional determination of human capacity having been made prior to any offer of address or attention. Tolerance may encourage the former attitude, indifference. Radicalism, however, encourages the latter, a manipulative interest, and it seems to me that in doing so it brings about a fundamental derangement of human relations; some assume that they themselves are righteous and knowing and that all others are both susceptible to and in need of being thoroughly remade. A tolerance coming from indifference at least preserves the possibilities of communication, whereas such possibilities are destroyed by a manipulative interest. Hence the cruelty and suffering associated with efforts at revolutionary reconstruction, as in Russia, are not due to accidents of personality; it is not true that other men in the positions of revolutionary command might have achieved the humane ends of the revolution. On the contrary, this cruelty and suffering are inherent in an initial severence of communal relations.

Tolerance does not necessarily mean acceptance of injustice but only unwillingness to initiate an attack on it by abandoning receptivity. A tolerant radicalism might refuse to be involved in any reformist or revolutionary activity that seriously imperils possibilities of communication. Such a refusal would require a good deal more restraint than is customary among radicals. It is not clear, however, that it would more seriously inhibit the attainment of radical aims than does the usual radical assumption that community can be reached only by temporarily precluding it.

These considerations, it seems to me, are neglected by Robert Paul Wolff, Barrington Moore, and Herbert Marcuse in their "critique of pure tolerance." [17] In questioning the significance of tolerance in America, Marcuse and his associates are at the very least plausible. But in arguing, or encouraging the reader to infer, that left-wing intolerance is therefore justified, they pay far too little attention to the corruption of human relations that is threatened by a suspension of tolerance. Of course, those whose grievances are serious, and who have no chance of being heard, cannot be expected to acquiesce in a fraudulent regime of tolerance. But should not their acts of violence be strictly limited to what is necessary for replacing "repressive tolerance" with communal and truth-seeking tolerance?

Marcuse and Wolff seem to feel that tolerance has no place in a society until elementary justice is established. From the standpoint I have been suggesting, however, that is a reversal of the proper order of things. Justice is not a condition of tolerance. Rather, tolerance precedes justice; it establishes the possibility of discussions through which members of a society may reach agreement as to what justice is and what it requires. Tolerance is the source of that interpersonal space within which practicing justice is not coldly rendering each one his due but rather is a matter of respecting the form of a living community.

This rejoinder to Marcuse can be put in terms of equality, which is not only generally assumed to be, in some form, indispensable to justice but is also usually the major goal of radical reform. Two kinds of equality must be distinguished. One is outward and observable, and is exemplified most clearly in equality of income, where equality is precisely measurable. This may be called "objective equality." The other kind of equality comes from recognizing that every individual possesses immeasurable worth. This kind of equality does not require complete objective equality, yet it does have an outward manifestation: I recognize the immeasurable worth of another by being willing to engage him in serious and unreserved communication. For this reason, the second kind of equality may be called "communal equality." The point I am leading up to is simple. Communal equality alone recognizes the dignity of man and is thus true equality; the attitude through which one establishes this equality is tolerance.

Radicalism will respond that communal equality, although it may be true equality, depends on objective equality. People cannot communicate if they are set apart from one another by drastic economic inequalities. Marcuse's argument, in essence, is that objective inequalities in America are such that communal equality is precluded; tolerance is consequently fraudulent. On these grounds, the use of violence is justified; objective equality must be forcefully created.

Questions concerning the use of violence in contemporary America—whether it is needed, what kind is likely to be fruitful, and so forth—are prudential, that is, to be answered only in the light of variable circumstances, and need not be taken up here. However, Marcuse's argument involves theoretical, as distinguished from prudential, questions that do concern us. Here everything turns on the issue of how much objective inequality there must be to justify violence. Marcuse does not specify; but he can be read as saying that violence is justified so long as there are objective inequalities that are seriously in conflict with the standards of justice. Has communication, then, no role in reaching justice? The truth, it seems to me, is that violence is justified only if objective inequalities are such that communal equality is barred. The test is the possibility of acts of address and attention that span economic gaps.

If there is to be communication of the utmost seriousness, after all, surely it must deal with questions of justice. Can there be a more fitting subject of communication? Yet justice is unlikely to be seriously discussed where it is already perfectly and securely established. This implies that justice is a possible issue of communication, but not a prerequisite. It is to express this idea that I suggest, at the risk of over-simplification, the formula that tolerance is prior to justice.

This formula does not rest merely on the notion that communication provides a proper means for reaching justice, however. It is the only possible means for reaching morally significant justice. Presumably, justice is the form of unity among human beings; that is, it is the form of community. But the substance of community, as has already been argued, is created by communication. Hence justice without communication, if it were possible, would be only a meaningless shell.

It may be that I misconstrue Marcuse. But it is evident that he does not recognize clearly the limits and dangers of intolerance. Interpreted broadly, his theoretical (as distinguished from prudential) argument is unexceptionable. Certainly, objective inequalities may be destructive of communal equality; in these circumstances tolerance is specious, and violence may be necessary to create the conditions under which tolerance can entail possibilities of community rather than just concealing irremediable alienation. But it needs to be seen that violence is so opposed to the spirit of tolerance that it is very difficult through violence to create the conditions of tolerance; if the end is tolerance, violence must be considered a treacherous—even if occasionally necessary—means. And, even at best, violence can establish only objective equality; whether this becomes a basis for communal equality depends on a spiritual act that no political contrivance can effect. In short, violence may well establish objective inequality—revolutionary despotism; but even if it establishes objective equality, it may not eventuate in community. My root disagreement with Marcuse is that he pays little attention to these considerations.

Insistence on the inseparability of receptivity and community, however, is only one aspect of the defense of tolerance against radicalism. This defense can be further developed by considering the second term of the concept of receptive realism. I suggest that typical radicalism is weakened not only by its lack of receptivity but by its lack of realism as well. Let us briefly consider the applicability to radicalism of each of the three principles discussed above.

1   *The risks of tolerance can be reduced through politics.* Despite their normal preoccupation with politics, radicals frequently evince a will to abolish politics. Thus they anticipate elimination of the conflicts that occasion politics and look toward "the withering away of the state." Resort to violence, and praise of revolutionary dictatorships, have like significance, often expressing a distaste for the process of negotiation and compromise that constitutes what most of us think of as politics. Of course, radicals usually hold that politics of this kind is counterfeit and conceals the dictatorial power of privileged groups. In some times and places this is undoubtedly true. The primary question, however, is whether it is possible under any circumstances to transcend the conditions of politics—that is, to progress beyond circumstances in which there is conflict, risk of injustice, and need for persuasion and compromise. The answer, if man is inherently unreliable, is that a world without politics is possible only if man can be reduced to an object of scientific knowledge and technological control. Radicals, of course, look for a new and more co-operative human species. But, aside from this hope, which has little to rest on, the willingness to put up with politics is inseparable from the willingness to put up with man as a mysterious and unpredictable creature.

Counterfeit politics would seem to justify revolution. Is there any humane and realistic goal for revolution, however, other than that of establishing a situation in which genuine politics is possible?

2   *If man is unreliable, then intolerance, as well as tolerance, is dangerous.* Radicalism has supplied a tragically unforgettable example that this is so in the figure of Joseph Stalin (a product of radicalism even if not, properly speaking, a radical himself). Through Stalin, an intolerant will to justice eventuated in a long reign of violent injustice. As I have acknowledged, radical disdain for tolerance is no doubt justified in some circumstances; when radical criticism has no chance of being considered and acted upon, then tolerance must be specious, a form without content. Often what radicals seek, however, is not a hearing but immediate and total acceptance of their views.

As a test for the legitimacy of violence, I suggest the following: first, that it be initiated only by or in behalf of people who have no opportunity of speaking and being heard; second, that it either offer reasonable prospects of making tolerance and community real, or else constitute in itself an act of communication. The purpose of violence is not to create a political work of art but to make communication possible—and tolerance thus significant. This may seem obvious, but I think radicalism has often been insensitive to the limits of action, and thus inclined to resort too readily to the most drastic means. But if communication is duly appreciated, and the incompatibility of communication and violence fully understood, then violence will be undertaken only under the spur of manifest, and tragic, necessity. And it will be undertaken only with "fear and trembling." All of this was recognized by Locke, and movingly expressed, in his references to revolution as an "appeal to Heaven."

3 *A perfect society is probably unattainable.* Most radicals believe that they themselves, acting at a propitious historical moment, not waiting to present arguments or listen to objections, could lay the foundations of a good society, if not a perfect one. It must be admitted that centralized, unhesitating power has had a place in historical progress. But the example of Soviet tyranny is relevant here as well; it indicates not only that there are far worse societies than tolerant societies but that these may ironically be brought into being by perfectionists for whom mere tolerance is not enough. People often recoil from utopian plans, and, I think, with good reason: a perfect society cannot be constructed without divesting men of their capacity for evil, that is, their unreliability, and we do not know how to do this while leaving them human. The faith of earlier, more Christian times that a perfect order would finally be created by God, although widely regarded as mere superstition, was more more realistic than radicalism usually is, for it recognized that such a task is not human.

Certainly, it is dangerous for anyone who lives comfortably and safely within an unjust order to become reconciled to the imperfection of all historical structures. What he thinks is wise resignation before human limits may be in fact only the way he conceals from his own conscience his contented acceptance of special privileges. Selfishness can utilize any moral posture.

The test, I suggest, is whether tolerance is upsetting—to the tolerant individual and to society. It is a bad sign when tolerance is accompanied by contentment. A tolerant individual should find that it is hard to reconcile himself to the imperfections of men and

societies and that receptive realism is disagreeable. A tolerant society should find that it cannot simply listen to its critics and continue as before but that established powers, institutions, and assumptions are continually placed in question. In short, tolerance should
mean dissatisfaction for individuals and disturbance for societies.
To say this, however, is to anticipate the two final chapters of this
essay, and consequently this observation does not need to be elab-
orated upon here.

3

To sum up the general theme of this section, historical pessimism
forces us to reinterpret, not to discard, tolerance. Thus reinterpret-
ed, tolerance involves a certain kind of relationship with evil—a relationship in which one neither accepts it nor takes its destruction
for granted. That is realism. Tolerance is receptive as well when
evil is not allowed to dictate the assumption that nothing new or
good can be hoped for on the part of man.

This theme parallels those of the preceding two sections, concerning the communal and transrational convictions that have developed in recent times. In each section I have tried to assess the
meaning, for tolerance, of attitudes very different from those on
which the idea of tolerance first was founded. And I have suggested in each section that the new attitudes do not undermine tolerance but rather provide it with new support and new meaning. The
upshot of my argument, then, is that not only is it still possible to
be tolerant; it seems that we need to learn a different kind of tolerance from that of the past.

Summarily, to contrast this tolerance with the traditional tolerance I have been criticizing, it may be said that tolerance is no
longer expediency. For Locke and Mill, and I believe for most liberals, tolerance is desirable on grounds of its beneficial consequences. As I have acknowledged, there are many intimations in Locke
and Mill of a different view; but the substance of their case consists largely in an estimate of consequences that finds tolerance
pragmatically valid.

The idea we can now envisage is that tolerance is inherently
receptivity toward persons and toward the truth. It may have unpleasant consequences; it may lead to something other than community, truth, and historical progress. But tolerance in itself is a
communal and truthful state; hence to abandon it does not bring

us to the goals we seek. Its dangers have to be accepted. In the traditional view, tolerance is a way of gaining benefits; in the present view, it means running risks.

To be tolerant is to approach being in a different way then when assessing consequences. It is to enter the sphere of persons and of truth, which is a sphere of communication rather than of artifice and calculation. To be sure, in confronting the consequences of tolerance it may be necessary to become involved in artifice and calculation. But this is only because of an initial decision to run the risks of facing toward being with attentiveness and with openness.

On our capacity for doing this may depend our keeping a humane and civilized balance amid the doubts and tragedies of the twentieth century. We are tempted to violence both by impatience and by despair. We are tempted to look on men with contempt either because they persistently fall short of perfection or because we come to doubt the very premise underlying the hope of perfection—that there is a difference between good and evil. The ideal of tolerance calls for a lot less than perfection but perhaps for more than we can provide in coming decades. Radicals are certainly right in feeling that man should be more than merely tolerant, but the danger is that he will be less.

May I remind the reader, however, that this essay does not purport to offer a complete theoretical solution to the problems it poses. To borrow phrases used at the end of the preceding chapter, its aim is that of exploring possibilities and sketching outlines. I shall proceed to do this by considering the new concept of tolerance, first in its general temper, and then in its implications for the organization of society.

III Tolerance as Suffering

ACCORDING TO THE traditional liberal view, tolerance is natural and easy. The tone of the *Letter Concerning Toleration* is one of serene common sense. Although the idea of toleration was not generally accepted in the seventeenth century, Locke writes as though a sensible person will be tolerant as a matter of course, as soon as the advantages of that attitude have been pointed out to him. Mill's tone was angrier than Locke's, perhaps because he was writing almost two centuries later, when it was possible to suspect in man a perverse tendency to persist in intolerance even after its absurdity had been shown. No more than Locke, however, does Mill suppose that tolerance might be difficult and trying even for an enlightened person. A similar attitude is evident today in the incredulity and outrage with which liberals typically regard acts of intolerance. For them, as for Locke and Mill, tolerance is clearly and simply the only rational attitude one can have toward others.

To set aside the individualism, rationalism, and historical optimism that characterized the traditional conception of tolerance, however, is to do away with the notion that it is natural and easy. Tolerance must now be seen as a form of resistance to strong and elemental impulses and to be in that sense anti-natural. It must be seen as onerous and demanding, rather than easy. Communalism, transrationalism, and historical pessimism do not bar tolerance; on the contrary, as I have argued, they require it. But they do bar a tolerance that is practiced because it seems to be uncomplicated and profitable.

THE BURDENS OF TOLERANCE

If tolerance is to survive, I suggest that its temper must become resolute and sometimes even grim. Not only was Locke a tacit, and Mill an avowed, utilitarian; but most English and American liberals as well have been, consciously or unconsciously, utilitarians. For utilitarians, happiness is the highest goal—and tolerance traditionally has been seen as contributing to it. In contrast, it seems to me that the tolerance now called for must be seen as an unhappy tolerance. This may seem to be an exaggerated phrase, and it is true, of course, that the utilitarian view cannot simply be reversed, with tolerance conceived of as no more than a cause of misery. If man seeks community and truth, and gains access to these only through tolerance, then to be tolerant is to move toward the complex joy of participating in being. This joy might be called "happiness." But it is a mixed and demanding happiness—one not likely ever to be enjoyed in a pure state and one bound to be costly in terms of patience and endurance.

The unhappiness of tolerance can be seen in connection with each of the principles through which tolerance was interpreted in the preceding chapter.

Communalism   It is apparent from the vantage point of this principle that to be tolerant is to endure estrangement. Communal tolerance comes from the realization that unity cannot be willed or imposed. People must be allowed to stand off from one another and then to cross freely the distance separating them. Community is possible only in that way. Tolerance is provisional acquiescence in interpersonal distance. It reflects a willingness for others to be unsettling, incomprehensible, even repellent. This attitude is dictated by the hope of community and truth, but the fulfillment of this hope may be long delayed or even completely denied. Where there is full community, no tolerance is necessary. Tolerance becomes essential where one must await the other, in his veracity and responsibility. The tolerance I have tried to sketch in this essay is a simultaneous refusal of total separateness and of the kind of unity that can be seized and held. To be tolerant is to be separate without entertaining the comforting delusion that separateness is good in itself.

For Locke and Mill, tolerance was in principle, if not always in application, a state of detachment natural and proper to man. This state was not one of estrangement, properly speaking, for one is not estranged from that with which he has no desire or need to be united. Tolerance was not difficult because it was in essence a matter of settling into relations of mutual indifference; the perplexities and trials of communication could be left to one side.

A concern for community imposes more complex obligations. Community ensues from a dialectic of estrangement and reconciliation. This is a requirement imposed by human nature. Only if man were, like a rock, an entity which simply is what it is, with no freedom and no divergence between essence and actuality, could community be a stable unity like that of a collection of rocks making up a wall. As it is, no relationship is communal without being recurrently attenuated and restored. Community is an insecure and incomplete conquest of estrangement, and men can only pursue it like partisan fighters trying to gain possession of their homeland.

The starkest symbol in Western culture of the relation between estrangement and community is Jesus on the Cross. All of the actions and words of Jesus' life, according to the New Testament, were determined by selfless love; his single motive was that of communicating the truth. In his love, therefore, he was at one with all. In his actual destiny, however, he was separated from all, hated and mistrusted by many and abandoned even by his disciples. The purest love required the most complete and tragic estrangement. Thus a man hanging on a cross paradoxically became the symbol of universal love.

Tolerance—when it is communal and not individualistic—manifests recognition of the strange conjunction between estrangement and community. It is an acceptance of estrangement, not as Locke and Mill accepted it, as normal and advantageous, but as a cross unavoidably borne by communal man.

Transrationalism   A tolerant person must be burdened not only with estrangement but also with doubt. He refuses the immediate and comfortable certitude made available by dogma and admits that the truths on which he relies most heavily may not be truths at all, and that even at best they are not true in a way that precludes their being replaced by more comprehensive, or simply different, formulations. He does this, of course, in order to understand reality, which may be clarified by doctrines but not enclosed within them—reality that is of such a nature as to be more fully present in a truth that is questioned than in a truth that is purportedly final. Like Socrates, he is looking for the knowledge that lies in ignorance. His uncertainty is a burden, however, even though it is accepted in the hope of gaining access to reality. For most of us, our esteem for ourselves, as well as our sense that we have a definable place in a comprehensible world, is tied up with "truths" we do not seriously question. These give us a sense of knowing where we are and what we are about. But such assurance is lost when these "truths" are thrown into doubt. For most of us, ignorance is a form not of insight, as it was for Socrates, but of humiliation and disorientation.

It cannot be denied that Mill and the many liberals who have shared his viewpoint have explicitly demanded that man take on the burden of doubt. They have seen that burden, however, as one that by being borne becomes steadily lighter and finally disappears. This makes it very different from the Socratic uncertainty that tolerance requires. A traditional liberal accepts doubt merely in order to destroy it; thus Mill believed that, by admitting how unsure we are, we embark on an intellectual journey that will lead finally to a comprehensive science of man. Simply stated, rationalist tolerance requires only provisional uncertainty. In contrast, transrationalist tolerance requires that one accept uncertainty as the inalterable atmosphere of life. Truth is found within uncertainty, not by destroying it.

I pointed out in the preceding chapter that to accept uncertainty is to make room for the other; it is to grant the possibility of there being persons with insights different from mine. Correspondingly, to endure the pain of uncertainty is a kind of readiness for enduring also the pain of estrangement. The opinions of the other may be completely different from anything I had anticipated and, in the light of my own understanding, absurd. As a result, the one who holds those opinions is apt to appear either threatening or contemptible.

Historical pessimism   According to traditional views, tolerance at least would bring no losses, and it would be a likely source of gains; since men are rational and co-operative, it would usually release constructive forces. Historical pessimism, however, rules out such confidence. If men are unreliable, then tolerance is dangerous. For Mill, the mood of tolerance was one of expectancy; a tolerant society could look forward to drawing ever nearer to the truth and to social harmony. The mood of contemporary tolerance must be one of historical anxiety.

This contrast can be illustrated with well-known examples from ancient history. It can be seen in retrospect that the Athenians, by opening their public life to whatever words and actions might come forth from an energetic and ingenious people, entered on a national career destined to be glorious, but also short and troubled. Life in Athens must have been exhilarating, but it was insecure. Class antagonisms were fierce, governments were unstable, foreign policy was erratic; there were no encircling dogmas and institutions, and no ascendant authorities, exempt from doubt and rebellion.

This was not the situation in every city. Athens' long-time enemy, Sparta, was admired even by many Athenians for a changelessness that made it seem as though man had overcome time. No doubt a Spartan could count on the future in a way that an Athenian could not, and in the Peloponnesian War Spartan discipline was finally victorious. The Spartan, however, had to go without freedom in order to enjoy the reassuring stability in which his life was encased.

I pointed out above that in recommending tolerance, Locke and Mill did not appear to be fully cognizant of the consequent problems of political control, and that this was because their optimism obscured the risks inherent in tolerance. Indeed, considering their trust in spontaneous harmony, a harmony coming from human rationality and co-operativeness as well as from natural forces reconciling even irrationality and selfishness, it is hardly too much to say that through tolerance, in their view, man partially divested himself of political responsibility. If historical optimism is rejected, however, then tolerance has to be looked upon as magnifying the weight of political responsibility. Tolerance is likely to be a source of uncertainty and conflict and in this way places heavy demands on political sagacity and foresight.

Finally, pessimistic intolerance entails the discomfort of lowered hopes. Tolerance does not open the gates to the good society but only to a society better than the worst. Some of the most stirring, and at the same time disappointing, chapters in the political history of the past two centuries have come from anticipations of political and social transfiguration. As I have already indicated, and as I will make more explicit in the following chapter, tolerance is not equivalent to conservatism; it means a willingness to criticize the past and to challenge the authority of tradition. But it does not pretend to grant man an assured future to take the place of the crumbling past. It offers only a future that is undecided.

The burdens of tolerance, then, are estrangement, uncertainty, and historical insecurity. But not only are these unpleasant in themselves; to accept them involves a difficult act of self-contradiction. One takes on estrangement out of concern for community, accepts uncertainty from love of truth, and liberates men whom he mistrusts. José Ortega y Gasset once referred to liberalism as "acrobatic." [1] This is a word that perfectly describes the attitude of tolerance, once it is taken out of the individualistic, rationalistic, and optimistic framework in which it first was set. Tolerance must combine love and detachment, understanding and doubt, trust and suspicion. The tolerance recommended by Locke and Mill corresponded in a direct and non-paradoxical fashion to man's nature and desires. For them, men were basically separate, and tolerance recognized this fact; men desired truth and through tolerance they would reach it; they sought order and progress and tolerance was the pathway to these values. Traditional liberal tolerance, in short, is not at all acrobatic. Thus it is far easier and more agreeable than the tolerance that now seems to be required of us.

I suspect that tolerance depends ultimately on one of the most mysterious and difficult of human acts, that of forgiving. I am not suggesting a strictly logical dependence: one may, without inconsistency, tolerate actions he cannot forgive, just as he may forgive actions he would not tolerate. Rather, the dependence is psychological. It is doubtful that one can accept another, who is strange, who jeopardizes his beliefs, who may contribute to social disintegration, without confidence that he can forgive whatever evil is actually done. Mercy renders evil tolerable without palliating it. It distinguishes between the person and the evil he has done and in this way curbs the self-righteousness and impatience that often makes men of high moral standards hungry for violence. This is why it may be the key to a tolerance that is realistic but not complacent.

Saying this, however, is another way of emphasizing the difficulty of tolerance, for the same terms applied to tolerance—"onerous," "anti-natural," "acrobatic"—can be applied equally well to forgiveness. In forgiving, one overlooks evil without denying or ignoring it. Real forgiveness cannot occur unless one is conscious that evil is without justification, that it forbids man to rest but demands in some way to be wiped out or counterbalanced. Forgiveness nevertheless allows the evil to pass and to be forgotten.

Nature impels man toward retribution. Thus highly cultivated and intelligent peoples like the Greeks had scarcely any concept of forgiveness. Christianity (not alone among religions) has, of course, stressed the duty of forgiveness; but nature has held its own against religious doctrine, for even in so consciously Christian an era as the Middle Ages penal practices were often bloody and vindictive in the extreme. The urge to punish can claim authority as a natural desire, a social necessity, and a moral imperative.

Forgiveness involves the difficult and dubious act of defying all such authority.

In sum, through the capacity to forgive, one covers in advance the evil that tolerance may permit; but the source of this capacity is unclear. Forgiveness, and thus tolerance as well, involves the unnatural and even illogical act of passing over evil even while regarding it with utmost seriousness.

If tolerance is always onerous and demanding, it is probably particularly so in the twentieth century, when the normal consequences of tolerance—estrangement, uncertainty, and historical insecurity—seem particularly menacing. In some periods, such as the twelfth century in Europe or the nineteenth century in England, people seem to have felt an undergirding of community, belief, and order. Today we do not. We feel that the individual is in danger of total estrangement, that every belief may collapse, and that the very continuance of the human race is in doubt. Thus a common symbol of what we sense about us is the abyss. This situation probably has much to do with the rise of totalitarianism. Men draw together in horror and try with violence to forge the undergirding of community, belief, and order that once seemed to be a gift of nature or of God.

What I have tried to do so far in this chapter is simply to show that tolerance must usually be burdensome. This suggests a way of understanding the essence of tolerance.

BEARING OTHERS

The word "tolerance" is related to Latin and Old English terms meaning to lift up and to bear. I suggest that the fundamental nature of tolerance is indicated by this etymological background.

Tolerance is bearing, or suffering, the conditions introduced by others. These conditions have been summarily described in the preceding section: they are estrangement, uncertainty, historical insecurity, and a divided mind (divided between love and the allowance of distance, understanding and doubt, trust and suspicion). All of these conditions keep one from enjoying self-sufficient, secure, and simple personal existence. As a communal creature, man neither desires to, nor can, exclude others from his attention and life; no person can be wholly indifferent to any other person. Yet most of these others—all of them, in some measure—are strange;

they are truly *others*, not simply manifestations of the self, as the depersonalizing Hegel maintained. And not only are they strange. They often understand man and his duties in different and unsettling ways, and they are frequently resentful and violent. The ideal of tolerance requires that these burdens be accepted and borne.

To bear, however, is not only to suffer but also to support or uphold. If tolerance is communal, it must be understood as bearing others in this sense too. A human being is sustained by the sympathetic interest of another. The interpretation of tolerance as communal implies that it must be a proffer of such interest. A tolerance that primarily expresses indifference, that allows each one to do as he pleases because others do not care what he does, is tolerance as Locke and Mill in principle conceived of it but not as it has been defined in this essay. One of the main reasons for tolerance is to permit the other to be present as he really is, veraciously and responsibly. Thus tolerance is senseless when it is merely a withdrawal of attention. It becomes a way of isolating the other— leaving him free, but in a void. A tolerant person "puts up with" others, but he does so attentively and thus upholds them. In suffering them, he provides the communal atmosphere in which freedom is significant because it contains opportunities for entering into authentic relationships.

Construed according to these two senses of the verb "to bear," the ideal of tolerance embodies some familiar, and elemental, truths concerning human relations. First, man brings suffering to man, not only through violence and other kinds of destructiveness, but through creativity and communality as well; some of the greatest men have been so unsettling to their contemporaries that they have been persecuted and killed. But further, man is bound to man by love; hence the suffering implicit in human relationships has to be deliberately endured. Finally, love must manifest itself by accepting the freedom of its object. Love is for persons, and persons are not, like works of art, subject to being made exactly what one would like them to be; hence love that becomes regulatory and manipulative destroys the possibility of its own fulfillment. The concept of tolerance as communal, transrational, and historically pessimistic is intended to reflect these principles.

This line of thought can be pursued further: tolerance involves recognition of something man would gladly forget—his finitude.

In this sense, tolerance is an acknowledgement of the human condition. Let me try to explain the logic of this acknowledgement. To say that man is finite is to say that much is beyond his knowledge and control; the consequence is vulnerability to various evils, of which the climactic evil is unavoidable death (in Job, "the king of terrors"). Man tries persistently to rise above his finitude by bringing all reality within the scope of his understanding and command; if this were fully accomplished, not only would life be pleasant but also death would be overcome. Modern man hardly feels obliged to apologize for this Promethean urge. However, it incorporates the hubris that the ancient Greeks condemned as heedlessness of human limits certain to eventuate in disaster; further, and more directly relevant to the present point, it incorporates the central Christian sin, that of withholding love. The aspiration toward sovereignty over all reality is necessarily loveless because its aim is the reduction of persons to objects known and controlled. In short, men try to flee from their finitude by dominating other men.

The dominated, of course, often resist. Their masters may temporarily forget their finitude in the enjoyment of their mastery; but those under them, through the insecurity and suffering of their servitude, have the consciousness of finitude forcibly impressed upon them. Their resistance, however, is not necessarily a flight from finitude. It may reflect a refusal to be objects and thus it may be an affirmation of personal being. The effect of servitude sometimes is to inspire an emphatic and courageous claim to dignity. Dostoevsky asserted that "the whole work of man really seems to consist in nothing but proving to himself every minute that he is a man and not a piano-key"; to accomplish this, he held, man would "contrive sufferings of all sorts" and would "launch a curse upon the world." [2]

What men do through such rebellions is to force their masters back into a recognition of their own finitude and their guilt in trying to rise above it. They prove relative and incomplete the knowledge that the masters wanted to hold as absolute and all-comprehensive; they do this by falsifying their predictions and disrupting their plans. They compel them in this way to acknowledge what they wanted to forget: the incalculable realms that lie beyond their comprehension and mastery. That is, they compel them to acknowledge their finitude.

The struggle may, of course, have no end. The rebels may in turn become masters and may have to be reminded of their finitude by the rebellion of others. Thus human beings may be continually embroiled with one another through trying to escape the humiliation and anxiety of being merely human.

Through tolerance, however, one brings the struggle to a close. The project of escaping from finitude is abandoned. In facing his limits, man views himself as only one among many, and in this way he grants, as it were, a place in the universe for others. Conversely, in accepting the right of others to express themselves in all of their disturbing reality, he resigns himself to his finitude.

This is merely to extend a theme outlined in the preceding chapter. There I argued that accepting the independent and unknowable being of the other was a resignation of one's own claim to complete and certain knowledge. Here I am suggesting that such a claim often expresses an effort to transcend finitude and that resigning the claim is thus an acceptance of finitude. I am suggesting also that when the latter is done a deep source of conflict is thereby closed. [3]

The tolerance recommended by Locke and Mill was basically different from the attitude I am sketching here. It entailed no necessity of bearing others, for each one inhabited a sphere where he might be largely ignored; and in any case he was rational, calculable, and co-operative. Thus tolerance was largely relaxation into a state of mutual detachment and harmony that was natural to man. It meant facing the human situation only by observing an order so agreeable that if man were sensible and enlightened he would never think of leaving it. Nor was tolerance for Locke and Mill an upholding of the other. The central meaning of traditional individualism was that the grounds of each man's being lay in himself. The aim of life suggested by the essay *On Liberty* is a uniqueness owing little to the support of others and not intended to elicit their interest or understanding. In the traditional view, to be tolerant was to be detached. That is very different from according the other a freedom one has to bear—to suffer and to uphold.

Having so sharply stressed the burdensome nature of tolerance, however, I feel obliged to ask—but not to answer—a question that causes discomfort, and even hostility, on the part of many people today. It concerns the ultimate grounds of tolerance. Is tolerance rational (that is, defensible in terms of any ultimate principle) if

beyond man there is no divine being such as the Good of Plato or
the God of Abraham and Moses? Many people today assume that
it is, and that religion and tolerance are mutually incompatible.
Even though this may be correct, however, the matter is not so
readily settled as many assume. Considering the mysterious and
paradoxical nature of tolerance, determining its ultimate grounds
cannot be simple or easy. The following reflections are intended
as an exploration of these grounds.

TOLERANCE AND THE SENSE OF ETERNITY

The kind of tolerance outlined in this essay depends on fidelity to
community and to truth. Tolerance is a difficult attitude to maintain, but one will do so—will bear others—in a measure corresponding to the strength of one's will to enter into community and to
understand the truth. But why should one desire community and
truth? I have formulated my arguments as though man obviously
does and as though the question of why he should does not need
to be raised. In short, I have based this discussion on the assumption that community and truth are objects of natural desire.

This assumption, I think, is valid. As Plato and Aristotle, as
well as many succeeding thinkers, have argued, man strives continually to get in touch with full and enduring being. In himself, man
is fragmentary and ephemeral; deprived of relationships he feels
overwhelmed by nothingness. Thus he is driven toward participation in a reality more inclusive and more lasting than himself. This
is not to deny that man is driven also to assert his own interests at
the expense of others. Doing this expresses the same recoil from
nothingness as does the drive toward community. But self-assertion
is ultimately abortive. Man depends on his relationships not just
for his biological life but for his spiritual life as well; his very identity as a human being—parent, neighbor, employee, etc.—is established by the relationships he sustains. His pride and egotism,
therefore, are in conflict with the deepest needs of his nature—
needs that can be satisfied only through community and truth.

So brief a statement necessarily passes over many complexities
and possible questions. My aim here is not to overcome all doubts,
but only to state explicitly an assumption that has been made in
the course of the preceding arguments: that the relationships gained
gained through communication and through apprehension of the

truth are objects of natural desire. The one thing that seems to be required at this point is to ask what kind of demands the desire for community and truth places on the universe and whether a universe without divine ground or governance can meet those demands.

Two such demands are discernible. These can be phrased as postulates that must be veridical for the pursuit of community and truth to succeed.

1   *Each person deserves respect.* We express this idea when we speak of "the dignity of the individual" or of man as "an end, and not merely a means." It is probably impossible to give any rational account of what quality it is that commands respect, and I shall not try to do so here. It is sufficient to point out that commonplace phrases like those above show that most of us assume there is such a quality and, more important, that the realization of community depends on discovering it. One may find community in various kinds of relationships—family, work, study, and so forth. But although the outward occasion is variable, at least one thing is invariable—one can realize a communal relationship only with a person one respects. Now, the will to community is universal; whereas a few friends can be sources of deep satisfaction, all estrangement is painful and one desires unity with all mankind. Such a statement may sound extreme, but the moral traditions of the Greeks, the Jews, and the Christians indicate that it is valid; all of these traditions envision an underlying or ultimate unity of all human beings. It follows that the will to community is a will to find in every person the dignity that would make him a possible associate, and that to encounter a person whom one cannot respect is to suffer an injury that is serious and painful, though most people are so accustomed to such injuries that they hardly notice them. There is evidence supporting this viewpoint in the durability of the idea of human dignity in this age of spiritual disintegration. At a time when most of our certitudes have been lost, or exuberantly discarded, we cling to the idea that the individual is sacred. It would be nearly unbearable, as the agony of Nietzsche demonstrates, to discover that all human beings, or even most of them, are truly contemptible.

2   *Being deserves reverence.* This principle sanctions the search for truth. Whereas most people today assume that the truth is valuable simply because it is useful, the state of the world after several centuries of scientific progress shows that this is not unqualifiedly so. Moreover, the devotion to truth evinced in the lives of great

philosophers, scientists, and artists is not dependent on calculations of utility; that devotion seems to be based on a reverence for being that is manifest in a reverence for truth regardless of its consequences. No doubt the truth is often, perhaps even usually, useful. The love of truth, however, comes from a sense that the reality to which truth gives access is in itself a source of delight and composure.

It is possible that other postulates as well are involved in the search for community and truth. The identification of these two, however, is sufficient to enable us to proceed with the inquiry.

Departing from the two postulates above, I shall trace a line of argument leading to a conclusion diametrically opposed to prevailing ideas concerning the relationship of tolerance and religion. My object, however, is not to convince the reader of the conclusion but rather to underscore the question. The purpose of the argument is only introductory; it is intended to open up an area of inquiry that cannot be entered in this essay but of which the reader should be aware because of its proximity to the question as to the ultimate grounds of tolerance. The argument may be set forth in four steps.

The first step is to hold that both of the above postulates are contrary to observable facts. As for the first postulate, there are no empirical grounds for holding that each person deserves respect. Human beings are of uneven worth. A few of them deserve respect, but a number have shown themselves capable of horrifying irresponsibility and cruelty. The vast multitudes in between the good and the evil, if not as contemptible as they seemed to Plato and to Nietzsche, certainly do not display to an accurate and unsentimental observer qualities that compel us to consider each one of them as sacred. Great pagan intellects like Thucydides and Aristotle, unaffected by Stoic and Christian (both religious) notions of human brotherhood, did not discern a dignity reposing in each person.

It would be easy to be more sweepingly skeptical—to note, for example, that even the worth of "great men" is usually ambiguous and arguable. It could be noted also that not only each individual but probably the whole human race is destined for eventual extinction, thus throwing into doubt the final significance both of humanity as a whole and of its most distinguished representatives.

As for the other postulate, that being deserves reverence, there is no compelling reason to think that this is so. It is true that Plato, Aristotle, and other philosophers believed that ultimate being is a perfectly harmonious order and is not only, as it were, man's true home but also a pattern for the regulation of his soul. But this was more nearly a premise than a conclusion; they did not demonstrate its truth and could not possibly have done so. Today, being is commonly, and with equal justification, looked upon very differently. It is often regarded as a mechanism man can control and use, or else as horrifyingly indifferent to human interests—"absurd," as Albert Camus called it. Reverence for being gains no more support from dispassionate observation and reasoning than does respect for the individual.

The second step in the argument is to infer that within the universe disclosed by observation and reason the desire for community and truth can at best be only partially fulfilled. The will to community runs aground on the disappointing absence of dignity in most human beings as they actually are; the will to truth brings into view, beneath the things around us, indifferent mechanisms, absurdity, or even a void. In short, the universe does not meet the demands we place upon it. The position one falls back on depends on what kind of demands he thinks the universe is able to meet. Thus Plato, desiring community but having no notion of the "dignity of the individual," sketched an ideal society in which perfect unity would be realized only by a few philosophers crowning a hierarchy of human types; far from sharing truth with the multitudes of ordinary people, they would govern them with the aid of "noble lies." Plato respected some men, but not all men, and he revered being. Nietzsche exemplifies a more extreme alternative; he respected very few men and looked on being with horror rather than with reverence. The result was a glorification of the "will to power," manifest in the subjection of being, with this will fully realized only by "supermen"—by individuals who had risen above the established criteria of humanity.

The third step is to conclude that if reality is wholly natural, which is to say godless and consisting in nothing but things discoverable through observation and reason, then tolerance is baseless. The whole case for tolerance, in this essay, has been built on the twin foundations of community and truth. If the universe is such that these values are, at least for most people, altogether unreachable, the ideal of tolerance necessarily collapses. One might possibly call for tolerance among philosophers, or "supermen," or the members of some other special group, depending on the general philosophical position adopted. One might even call for tolerance in relation to the masses on some expediential grounds, such as the need for knowing what they are thinking in order to control them. But one could hardly recommend the unreserved attentiveness and openness that constitute the kind of tolerance outlined in this essay.

The fourth step of the argument is to point out the possibility of an alternative position, that of refusing to accept as final the verdicts of observation and reason. Many men, by no means unintelligent or uncritical, have had what may be called, in order to cover a variety of inner states, a "sense of eternity." They have felt assured of a divine and enduring reality beyond the world about them. The grounds for their assurance have ranged from overwhelming mystical experiences, such as those reported by Plotinus, to what may seem, in the case of a thinker like Kierkegaard, to be a pure act of will. The object of this faith has in some instances been conceived of as a personal entity who could be addressed by man, in other instances as an impersonal source of reality, like "the Good" in Plato; it has even been identified with the universe itself. Certain Buddhists have emphasized the indescribability of the eternal so relentlessly that they have often been taken to be atheists. The sense of eternity has many forms.

What makes it relevant to the subject of tolerance is that it usually bestows sanctity on men and on being. It may do so rather selectively, as can be seen in the ancient Hebraic conviction that the Jews were a "chosen people" or in the Christian doctrine of predestination. But exclusions of this kind are always precarious in religious consciousness; thus Jewish messianic expectations came to embrace all of mankind, and Christianity has tended always to dignify each person in spite of the predestinarian inclinations of some of its advocates. Likewise, the sense of eternity sometimes has prompted men not to revere being but to turn away from it in disgust. But it is illogical to abhor that which originates in the divine. Hence the norm is that reflected in the philosophies of Plato and Aristotle, Augustine and Aquinas, and contemporary Protestant thinkers like Paul Tillich: the sense of eternity carries with it a sense of the grandeur of all being.

The conclusion to which these four steps lead is that the respect for each person and the reverence for being on which tolerance depends become reasonable only in the context of a world-view determined by the sense of eternity. The demands refused by the natural universe are met from beyond that universe.

This argument takes its departure from a moral question, whether community and truth are ultimate values? It would be possible to construct a parallel argument setting out from a question of practicality, that is, whether tolerance is feasible if human affairs are subject to no divine oversight or assistance. It is not necessary to do this; a few comments will make the general character of this argument clear to the reader who has in mind the four steps of the preceding argument. It would run as follows.

Whether or not persons and truth should be regarded as ultimate values, in fact they are not so regarded; the world of actual human relations is determined largely by power and deceit. As a result, pure fidelity to the dignity of persons and to the truth puts a group or individual at a serious disadvantage. Tolerance, however admirable it may be, is always bound to be defeated if it depends wholly on man. The only alternative to this conclusion—which corresponds to the final step in the argument above—is that the risk of tolerance is reasonable on the assumption that human decisions directed toward the ultimate good are furthered by a power beyond political calculation. The argument would be, in other words, that tolerance requires appeal to a sense that eternity not only validates the values toward which tolerance is directed but also in some fashion sustains those values in history.

So abstractly stated, the second argument may seem far-fetched. Since at least as early as Augustine, however, Western peoples have been disposed to assume that the good is not only a standard over history but a power within history; this disposition is apparent not only in Christians such as Augustine but in figures of the Enlightenment like Condorcet and Kant. The historical pessimism posited above bars belief in the kind of unambiguous, humanly propelled progress envisioned by Condorcet but not in the idea that those oriented toward the absolute good are in a more hopeful position than a skeptical reckoning of political probabilities might suggest. Such an idea could be provided with almost nothing in the way of rational proof, but it could not be disproven either.

At the present time, to appeal from political dilemmas to religious faith strikes most people as violating good sense and even good taste. I set forth these possible arguments, however, not in the hope that they will be accepted but rather in the conviction that the issue to which they relate should be considered. The traditional concept of tolerance has been weakened not only by individualism, rationalism, and historical optimism, but also by a thoughtless agnosticism and atheism (I do not mean to suggest that agnosticism and atheism are always thoughtless). It has come to be assumed that serious religion is bound to be intolerant and that tolerance can only be expected from the kind of scientific and irreligious mind typified, brilliantly and sensitively, by John Stuart Mill. This dogmatic secularism has been an obstruction to social thought. It has obscured the range of spiritual possibilities, and thus of theoretical options, and in this way has tended to dissuade us from thinking about the ultimate bases of tolerance.

For example, it is assumed by many among both the religious and the irreligious that the sense of eternity must necessarily be embodied in some kind of dogma. Of course, it often has been; and the usual consequence has been intolerance. But one of the few prominent themes running throughout the Old Testament is the condemnation of idolatry—of the worship of gods made by men. Is not a dogma an idol, and is not dogmatic religion thus a kind of idolatry? That this is so has been maintained by at least one great religious thinker—Martin Buber.[4] What this idea suggests in reference to the subject of this essay is that tolerance particularly befits the sense of eternity by weakening and obstructing man's persistent impulse to bow down before his own dogmas. Correspondingly, it suggests that an authentic sense of eternity is inherently tolerant because it relativizes all human institutions and truths.

Another theoretical option may be noted in connection with the common present-day conviction that man has "come of age" and that any feeling of religious dependency is consequently anachronistic. A liberal of Mill's type is apt to assert that modern men, aside from a few who are swayed by nostalgia for a receding past, no longer feel much sense of eternity; he is further apt to point out that, on the whole, atheists and agnostics have perhaps shown a deeper appreciation of "the dignity of the individual" than have professed Christians. Is it possible, however, that humane atheists and agnostics are in reality not alienated from the eternal, while callous Christians are? Formal religious profession and worship may be less decisive regarding one's real orientation toward being than both believers and non-believers have generally taken it to be. It is Certainly one crucial test of religious consciousness is whether or not, in encountering another human being, one senses a dignity that is not revealed to dispassionate and skeptical observation.

In this section I have tried to ask, after describing the burdens of tolerance in the two preceding sections, on what ground one who bears these burdens stands. Among possible answers, I have outlined the one most at odds with the answer people today tend to give. My purpose has been to place the question in as high relief as possible. Through tolerance, we confront, and in some fashion accept, reality in its most trying form—that of persons who are strange to us, who dispute cherished beliefs, who imperil order and progress, and who, in doing all this, force us back into the finitude we would gladly escape. What is the ultimate faith and the ultimate hope underlying our willingness to undergo this confrontation?

In the final chapter, we shall consider realities that are easier to grasp. If tolerance is burdensome, it is unlikely to be practiced by many individuals outside of a social context that is favorable to it. Thus, having reflected on the stance of a tolerant person, we have to consider the nature of a tolerant society. In doing this, there will be an opportunity to take up a question which has several times called for an answer but which it has seemed advisable to postpone: what are the limits of tolerance?

IV The Tolerant Society

IN THE ESSAYS of Locke and Mill, attention is focused almost exclusively on the ideal of the tolerant individual. Of course, the tolerance of governments and other groups was important to both writers and implicit in their thinking, and their reflections on constitutional and representative government concerned in effect the institutions of a tolerant society. But, when they directed their attention to the specific question of tolerance, they seemed largely to forget social conditions and institutions. They did not seriously ask what conditions and institutions might favor tolerance but simply urged tolerance on individuals—no doubt hoping that they would be heeded by individuals with power. This approach accorded with their basic attitudes as defined in the first chapter of this essay. As individualists, they had little appreciation of the degree to which people depend on others in attaining the kind of moral balance required for tolerance.

The theory of tolerance outlined in this essay, however, implies that it is not enough for tolerance to be widespread and enduring merely as an attitude on the part of individuals; it needs the support of institutions and social forms. If people are interdependent, if they are not very rational, and if they are not reliably co-operative, then it is vain to expect many individuals to be tolerant without encouragement from those around them and without support from conditions and structures in the surrounding society. The end remains that which the liberals envisioned—tolerant individuals. But our premises—communalism, transrationalism, and historical pessimism—compel us to consider a means to this end that the liberal thinkers could ignore, that is, tolerant societies.

In reflecting on the nature of a tolerant society, we pursue a line of thought first taken up in Chapter II. There, discussion of the problem of reconciling tolerance with human evil gave rise to the idea that the viability of tolerance depends on politics. It was suggested that political artifice would be required for resolving conflicts ensuing from tolerance. But a politics of tolerance presumably would be concerned not just with settling immediate conflicts but also with more distant goals—with establishing enduring conditions that are conducive to tolerance and to communication.

Such conditions are the subject of the present chapter. We are concerned, then, with formulating political standards and counsel.

As soon as we try to define the nature of a tolerant society, however, we find ourselves led in a direction that for many will be unexpected, and even unwelcome, in a book on tolerance. If the final ends of society are community and truth, then society must aim at encouraging communication and inquiry. This introduces into the discussion questions concerning the order and unity of society rather than the independence of individuals—questions of a kind traditionally of greater interest to conservatives than to liberals.

TOLERANCE AND SOCIAL COHESION

The concepts of attentiveness and openness have been used, in preceding chapters, to denote a twofold personal orientation—toward other persons, and toward truth. These orientations do not differ in their general directions. Their objects can be conveniently envisioned as two concentric circles: the larger circle symbolizing persons, who cannot be comprehended intellectually and therefore are fellow inquirers rather than mere objects of knowledge, the smaller circle symbolizing truth, which, as a product of inquiry, develops and lives only in the space between persons. Thus attentiveness and openness are aspects of a single attitude. To be attentive toward a person is to be open to the truth of which he may be the source, and to be open to the truth requires personal attentiveness.

Some of the difficulties of tolerance can be described in these terms. Historical pessimism is called for not only because men are often malicious but also because they are frequently inattentive and closed. Perhaps most people, most of the time, have no active desire to hurt others; but they ordinarily have little awareness of others and little desire to become related to them through the truth. And, if tolerance is burdensome, owing both to its attendant historical risks and to the estrangement and uncertainty it entails, then so are attentiveness and openness, for they are the basic elements of tolerance.

This brings us to a very general understanding of the nature of a tolerant society. It is attentive and open. More specifically, it inclines its members to be attentive and open; to do this, it must bring them into relationship with one another, and it must do this continually and reliably.

Saying this introduces a note of "conservatism" into the discussion. The ideal of a tolerance at once communal and realistic points to the need for various kinds of secure, objective relationships, such as those found in an old, tradition-laden society. Those relationships are not in themselves communal, since community is not objective and cannot be secure. But community is impossible in the absence of outward bonds and assurances. I agree with those writers who feel that there is a danger to our very humanity in the notion, common among certain types of radicals, that if established relationships are simply destroyed perfect communities will spontaneously arise from the ruins. It is true, as has been frequently noted in this essay, that society and community are more or less antithetical; but it is equally true that they are inseparable.

What are the major characteristics, then, of an attentive and open society? The answer must be tentative. A complete and final answer would be what I referred to earlier in this essay as a "human absolute." It would specify, in a way that could not be added to or doubted, how society must be organized in order to be fruitfully tolerant. The idea is a contradiction in terms, for the absolute prescription would be destructive of the freedom on which tolerance depends. Subject to this qualification, however, four conditions seem to me particularly worth mentioning.

1   *Order*   This is the most obvious of the four, but, as many writers have shown, it is also elemental. Order divests human relationships of physical fear. Safeguards are established against robbery, injury, and violent death, thus creating space for community.

The idea of order is not quite so simple and innocuous as it may seem to be, however. Physical fear is not caused only by the prospect of being robbed, injured, or killed, and the order on which community depends can be disturbed in ways other than ordinary criminal assault. This point tells against the attitude toward order held by both the left and the right.

It tells against the left by directing attention to the fact that an act like shouting down a speaker is a form of physical assault and, as a disruption of order, tends to obviate the very possibility of the community that those who commit such acts often profess to be seeking. Radicals are often contemptuous of procedures. But procedures are essential to assure that the right to speak is secure not only against mobs but also against the established, behind-the-scenes powers often feared on the left. The goal of procedures is orderly communication.

The realization that disorder is not reducible to common crimes tells against the right by reminding us that fear for one's livelihood—for pay and job—is also a form of physical fear. So far as capitalism makes the meeting of basic physical needs dependent on the variable and arbitrary will of owners and managers, it is, as socialists charge, a type of disorder.

2   *Unity*   The difference between unity and community has been briefly indicated elsewhere in this essay; it is important here that the difference be clear. The word "community" denotes a relationship in which persons are freely and fully present to one another; thus it applies only to human beings and, in a limited fashion, to a few animals, such as dogs. The word "unity," on the other hand, denotes an impersonal relationship and may apply to any kind of complex objective reality; a stone wall, a tree, an army platoon, all manifest unity. The difference between unity and community is fundamental, and confusing them is dangerous, for the former can be created by force and deceit, whereas the latter depends on freedom and insight. Through terror and propaganda, dictators ostensibly seeking total *community* have created societies of such total *unity* that community was impossible; hence the paradox of tyrannies: monolithic unity joined with radical alienation. Nevertheless, community cannot come into being without unity. As an obvious illustration, people cannot speak with one another unless (setting aside special devices like interpreters and telephones) they are united by language and physical location. Without certain kinds of unity, human relationships are bound to be affected by indifference or hostility.

What kinds of unity are needed? Physical unity seems indispensable. Widely inclusive and enduring community has probably come nearest to being realized in cities such as ancient Athens and Renaissance Florence; physical proximity (these cities being small and walled in, with much of life carried on in public, outdoor places) seems to have played an important part in the spiritual achievement. Among the greatest obstacles to attentiveness and openness in America are the prevalence of separate, self-contained family dwellings and the absence of public meeting places like the sidewalk cafés in Europe.

Another kind of unity that seems indispensable is economic.
The communal potentialities of the Greek cities were never fully
realized because of the continuous class warfare occasioned by a
severe insufficiency of material resources. America, by contrast,
although not very attentive or open, has enjoyed considerable economic unity because its wealth has been not only great but also ex-
panding, making it possible for everyone steadily to get more without taking it from anyone else. In the eyes of Marcuse and Wolff,
of course, the inequities of the American economy are so drastic
that the consequent lack of economic unity undermines tolerance.
Whether they are right is not relevant at the moment. But in considering their critique of American tolerance it is important to distinguish between, on the one hand, the economic unity needed
for communication to be possible and tolerance thus significant
and, on the other, justice. The former might fall far short of the
perfect unity demanded by the standard of justice. It seems to me
that Marcuse and Wolff confuse the two. As a result, they identify
situations in which there is injustice but also possibility of communication with situations in which no communication between
those doing and those suffering injustice is possible. In this way,
they are led to an overly casual legitimation of left-wing intolerance. But if justice is not a prerequisite of communication, neither
is it a prerequisite of tolerance. Rather, as maintained earlier in this
essay, justice that is not mere remorseless righteousness depends on
tolerance. The prerequisite for tolerance, in turn, is sufficient economic unity to enable those separated by injustice still to address
and hear one another.

Finally, community depends on cultural unity such as that ef-
fected by a common language and literature. Shared symbols and
standards are the intellectual conditions of inquiry and of mutual
understanding. Various international tensions within the West,
such as those dividing France and Germany during the past century, however, show that cultural unity presents no more than a
possibility of community. Cultural unity, no less than physical
and economic unity, becomes communal only through being taken
as an occasion for attentiveness and openness.

3 *Spiritual transparency*   This phrase may sound suspiciously
"mystical," but it seems to me appropriate for designating the character of a society containing many reminders of ultimate meaning.
The reminders may be literary—Homer was a source of spiritual

transparency in ancient Greece; they may be architectural, like the
Greek temples and the Gothic cathedrals; they may be natural, as
is apparent in the experiences of Rousseau and others in the presence of lakes, forests, and mountains; they may even be political,
as can be seen in the traditional charisma ("divine gift") of kings.
Such symbols are not confined to one type of meaning; the vision
embodied in Homer was very different from that contained in the
New Testament, but both works have been sources of transparency
because both have directed men's minds beyond the things immediately before them. Nor are these various meanings apt to be specific and statable, such as those set forth in religious dogmas; anything literal is likely only to make the ultimate immediate, thus
destroying transparency. Karl Jaspers terms symbols of this kind
"ciphers," indicating in this way that their meanings are equivocal
and uncertain. They do not provide information, but remind us
that we are not, like animals, confined to the immediate. Usually
they suggest that all reality—even all that seems evil and senseless—
is somehow justified. But as "ciphers" they are cryptic, and in suggesting meaning they also ask about meaning. They do not tell us
what to believe so much as inviting us to decide what we believe.

Some of the ancient cities, with their temples and statues, and
with their proximity to the countryside and their openness to the
sunlight, must have provided a highly transparent environment.
Many medieval towns must have done so too, in view of their great
cathedrals, their dramatic and graceful secular structures, the human scale of their dwellings and streets, and the accessibility of the
natural world. Perhaps the nature of transparency can best be indicated, however, through an example of its opposite—opaqueness.
The United States today seems to offer, in the population centers,
an opaque environment. Ugly and filthy cities, a debauched and
relatively inaccessible natural environment, and the trivial and he-
donistic cultural atmosphere created by the entertainment and advertising industries all make for a world containing no intimations
of ultimate meaning, a world closed in on itself.

Attentiveness and openness are not likely to arise among those
who are not drawn, by anything in their environment, toward comprehensive understanding. Certain circumstances make people
strongly inclined to devote themselves wholly to the world right
around them. For example, economic pressures may confine them
to the physical environment, as was the case with the industrial

proletariat until recently; exhaustion and the distractions of prosperity may work in the same direction, as in America today. I suspect that the widespread concern with environmental quality, while expressed in terms of physical problems such as pollution of air and water, arises to a greater degree than is generally recognized from a spiritual anxiety. It stems from a feeling not just that our surroundings are becoming increasingly unpleasant and unhealthy but that they threaten us with a kind of spiritual suffocation.

Order, unity, and spiritual transparency constitute, as I have said, mere possibilities of community. Their significance depends on whether they are apprehended as such, thus becoming foundations for communication and inquiry. The fourth condition to be discussed is not on the same footing as the other three. It is necessary both for their existence and for their communal utilization. Order, unity, and spiritual transparency cannot come into being and last, nor can they become occasions for attentiveness and openness, unless a few members of a society assume responsibility for seeing that these things happen. There must be authority, and authority in turn depends on the attitude of the people.

4   *The spirit of deference*   This is not the same as submissiveness. It is critical, and thus conditional and responsible. The attitude of most Germans toward Hitler was far too emotional and unreserved to be called "deferential," and Hitler himself was not, properly speaking, in a position of authority. Possessing authority should not be equated with inspiring fear and hysterical adulation. The spirit of deference is a disposition to obey or believe persons who meet certain criteria; these criteria may have to do with qualities in the persons themselves, with procedures that have placed them in power, or with both. If there are criteria, however, deference is conditional and may be replaced by disobedience and disbelief.

Deference is a precariously balanced attitude, upset on one side by submissiveness, on the other by arrogance. While it is probably true, as is so often said, that men were overly deferential (more precisely, they were submissive) during the Middle Ages and the early modern era, during the past century or two the spirit of deference seems to have given way to arrogance. Deference remains in the relations of laymen with specialists, such as physicians, but it has been greatly weakened in the relations of the populace with political leaders and with those who might address them from a

standpoint of comprehensive truth. Although many celebrated figures have gained a kind of ascendancy by doing and saying things
certain to be popular, no one genuinely defers to them very much.
The decline of deference is due partly to the democratic idea that
the preferences and opinions of the masses constitute a standard
which "leaders" must serve but not question; but it is also reflective of capitalism, which first caused traditional political authorities to be displaced by industrial magnates and then prompted
these new powers, as the mass market developed, to accord absolute sovereignty (except where profits were endangered) to the
consumers. By now the very concept of deference is suspect.

This may be an important source of our troubles today, for
society depends heavily on two basic types of authority. It depends
on *political* authority for order and unity, conditions that are not
wholly natural: for them to come into being and reliably endure
requires artifice. Political contrivance is needed to compensate for
defects in rationality and co-operativeness.

Spiritual authority plays a part in realizing unity and spiritual
transparency; it is necessary if the potentialities inherent in such
conditions are to be actualized as community. Spiritual authority
is composed of those who are empowered, by a deference that is
often merely spontaneous and informal, not to act but to speak or
otherwise express themselves. Political authority, of course, may
speak, but its distinctive responsibility is to act. Today, artists,
writers, philosophers, scholars, and journalists may all be spiritual
authorities whereas during the Middle Ages and the Reformation
spiritual authorities were generally churchmen. The point is, however, that even among a handful of people serious communication
is unlikely unless someone leads, as Socrates did in the dialogues
reported by Plato. If, even among a few, community depends on
spiritual authority, how much more true this is in a nation. Today
in America, the place of spiritual authority has been pre-empted by
celebrities and entertainers who are scarcely aware that entertainment and communication are by no means the same.

In concluding the discussion of these four conditions, it might
be said that fruitful tolerance does not come about through careless liberation. Thought must be given to conditions that tend to
give liberty a communal and inquiring cast. Certainly order, unity,
spiritual transparency, and the spirit of deference do not constitute
a complete and invariable list of such conditions. They may at

least, however, mark out a path for reflection—a path leading beyond the liberal preoccupation with limiting society and the radical willingness to destroy it.

We must follow this path somewhat further before considering some of the more liberal and radical implications arising from the ideal of tolerance. To say that fruitful tolerance is not achieved through careless liberation is to suggest that tolerance may be limited. We must think about this.

THE LIMITS OF TOLERANCE

The principle that we are justified in being intolerant of all that destroys tolerance, and of all that destroys the conditions rendering tolerance productive of community and truth, seems to me unassailable in theory. True, it can be argued that in practice the principle is better ignored, for limitless tolerance can do no harm. The rationalism and historical optimism behind the traditional liberal concept of tolerance, and the assumption that tolerance was largely independent of social conditions, provide some foundation for such an argument. Little difficulty could be expected from a categorical rejection of all limits (although neither Locke nor Mill went this far). But this position becomes untenable once it is admitted that men cannot be counted on to use their liberty in rational and co-operative ways. It has to be granted that sometimes their liberty may have to be limited.

Not even tolerance is a human absolute. Some American liberals have tried to make it such by claiming that the First Amendment bars any restrictions whatever on speech and press. This is probably one of the most benign of all absolutes. Like any absolute, however, it is an effort to find refuge from uncertainty and tension in a human judgment that is placed beyond reconsideration or qualification.

If there are no human absolutes, however, then there are no absolute limits on tolerance. In other words, limits on tolerance must be purely circumstantial, and communication may be justifiably restricted only when this is necessitated by a particular historical situation. Thus, for example, the Supreme Court has been on solid ground in holding that limits might be placed on speech constituting a "clear and present danger" to the nation; it would have left that ground, however, had it held that certain kinds of speech, such as attacks on the president or on the Constitution, might be prohibited regardless of attendant circumstances.

The assessment of circumstances is prudential rather than theoretical. All that can be done here, accordingly, is to suggest some reasonable lines of prudential calculation.

It may be useful to begin with the matter of violence. As virtually everyone would admit, a society cannot be tolerant of robbery, vandalism, and murder, because these subvert one of the principal conditions of attentiveness and openness, namely, order. But if it is necessary to outlaw violence, may it not be legitimate in some circumstances to outlaw words leading to violence? Most people would grant that an inflammatory speaker who is inciting a crowd to some immediate act of violence can be rightfully restrained. Why not, then, the distributors of an inflammatory printed sheet or a fanatical radio speaker? Suppose that racial conflict in America were to become so intense as to bring the country to the verge of civil war, that a right-wing organization were to sponsor a radio program encouraging white people to commit acts of terrorism against blacks, and, finally, that the Federal Communications Commission were to bar that program from the air. I would not feel obliged by my belief in tolerance to protest that restraint. (Having said this, I am bound to admit that restraining left-wing propaganda might be justifiable in some instances too.) Further, if the advocacy of specific acts of violence can in some cases be legitimately barred, I do not see how it can be denied that glamorization of violence in general might likewise be barred without compromising the standard of tolerance. It is not apparent, for example, that a tolerant society must allow businessmen to broadcast television programs that make the beating and shooting of human beings seem like casual and attractive acts.

Closely related to the problems of tolerance created by the advocacy and glamorization of violence are those created by obscenity, for both violence and obscenity reduce human beings to bodies at the disposal of others. Liberals typically assume that violence is much more base than is obscenity. This is, of course, a complicated question; but I doubt that the most careful weighing of the two would permit us to discount the similarity lying in the fact that both depersonalize and, in depersonalizing, eradicate the mutual respect on which a communal tolerance must depend.

There is one substantial argument against all restrictions on obscenity, namely, that censors frequently cannot seem to tell the difference between uninhibited art and commercial filth; thus they have committed offenses against community and truth, as in outlawing *Ulysses*, *Lady Chatterly's Lover*, and *The Tropic of Cancer*. Although this argument is far from negligible, however, I do not think it is conclusive. Not even the insensitivity of censors is an absolute. France is a relatively restrictive country with respect to obscenity, yet the intellectual atmosphere is more stimulating there than in America. The London theater does not seem to have been seriously hurt by the fact that much has been barred from the stage there that has been permitted in America.

Discussing possible limits on tolerance brings before us what seems to me one of the most serious problems in America, the frivolity and baseness of most television programs. The origins of this problem, of course, lie not in uncompromising tolerance but in the uncompromising adherence to the idea of free enterprise that underlay the absurdly casual assumption that a spectacular new means of communication should be put in the hands of businessmen. The problem does bear on the subject of this essay, however, for probably nothing does more than television to create in America an opaque life environment. And while the problem is a product primarily of uncritical capitalism, we are not likely to solve it until we overcome the inhibitions stemming from an individualistic and anti-political tolerance. A hundred years ago, tolerance of that kind was perhaps plausible; but now, with the television networks monopolized by commerce and industry, it becomes apparent that tolerance is mere weakness and folly if it cannot take intelligent care of the conditions on which its value, and even its continuance, depends.

Liberals in the tradition of Locke and Mill are apt to feel highly uncomfortable when faced with suggestions such as these. Typically, they warn that any restriction on tolerance opens the way to its total denial. It is true, of course, that every limitation on tolerance is dangerous. That limitations may nevertheless be necessary is another factor contributing to the burdensome and demanding character of tolerance.

Until recently, we have not had to worry much about limiting tolerance in the United States. Not that we have been unfailingly tolerant; but our periods of intolerance have been due (the Civil War aside) more to fear and weakness than to necessity, and thus in retrospect they have seemed shameful. Due to a wisely designed political order, vast space and natural wealth, and other favorable conditions, order and unity have seemed to be gifts of nature more than products of political art. Tolerance has been relatively easy. But circumstances are changing. During the final decades of the twentieth century, American democracy probably will be tried more severely than at any other period, except, perhaps, that of the Civil War. We could lose our freedom not only by becoming hysterically and foolishly intolerant—a possibility discussed at the beginning of this essay—but also by not having the wit to limit tolerance when necessary in order to preserve its social and spiritual grounds.

To defend tolerance, then, is not to repudiate every conceivable limit on tolerance. It is not to turn tolerance into an imperative blind to the exigencies of historical institutions and circumstances.

If the principle of tolerance is not an absolute that authorizes one to ignore practicalities, however, neither can it be translated into mere conservative caution. If it means anything, it must mean liberating people—so far as possible all people—for communication. That process entails risks.

TOLERANCE AND LIBERALITY

If the aim of limiting tolerance is to preserve it, then limits should be instituted in response only to necessity, not to mere risks. Probably every serious utterance that is not ignored or misconstrued gives rise to emotion and thus to dangerous tendencies. The principle of permitting only speech that is completely safe would be a formula for totalitarianism.

Care should be taken also that the outrageous and the seriously threatening not be confused. Speech may be radically in conflict with true and basic moral standards, and even with reason, without on that account menacing the conditions on which tolerance depends. And, even though it provokes indignation, it may perform the important service of weakening the dogmatic complacency encrusting ethical standards and rational knowledge. Tolerance can hardly fulfill its function of placing people in the sphere of uncertainty, which is the sphere of personal relationships and of truth, unless it is upsetting. It is for statesmen who are tolerant but who also are capable of taking into account the qualifications that reality imposes on every principle to decide when the boundary between the upsetting and the threatening has been crossed.

Thus we may distinguish among the outrageous, the dangerous, and the mortally threatening. The outrageous may not be dangerous, and the dangerous may not be mortally threatening. Even the dangerous, I am suggesting, should be tolerated in some measure; the outrageous should be tolerated even more fully. Some examples may help us to reflect.

Arguments for the genetic inferiority of certain races, so far as these are made by geneticists, seem to me clearly to belong to the category of the outrageous: they are upsetting but, so far as I can see, they may be tolerated without limit. Geneticists arguing the inherent inequality of races have stronger claims to tolerance than do purveyors of pornography in that they address themselves to reason. Their methods, at least ostensibly, are scientific, thus inviting reasonable dispute and refutation. To be intolerant toward them them under these conditions compromises our relationship to the truth. It announces our determination to believe only what we approve of, not what reason requires.

More subtly, when we refuse to consider the possibility of inborn racial inequalities, we compromise our sense of the dignity of persons. Men are "equal" because of a mystery and nobility of personality that renders them incomparable. If one race were more intelligent than another (which seems to me unlikely, and if it were true it would probably be unprovable), it still would not follow that the more intelligent race would have superior dignity. Do we take the IQ scores of individuals within a single race as ultimate measures of personal worth? To suppose that a human being's standing as an end in himself, and not merely a means, can be affected by any objective measurement reflects a fundamental confusion (this is implied in saying that the individual is of *infinite* worth), and those who insist that measurement must disclose equality are as deeply confused as those who would challenge racial integration and justice on the grounds of supposedly objective inequalities.

Pornography, as I indicated earlier, seems to me a more serious matter. It challenges our awareness of personal dignity, and it does this in a way that brushes aside reason and defies refutation. The common liberal view that pornography does no harm, and that even if it did it would harm only the individual and hence is of no concern to society, is dubious in the extreme. If pornography undercuts our sense that every person is an end, and not merely a means, then it is dangerous, both to the individual and to society. Even so, it is not necessarily mortally threatening, and probably a great deal of it should be tolerated. For one thing, the danger of confusing pornography and art, and suppressing the latter, is thus obviated; for another, a possibility of communication is thus preserved. Pornography need not always stifle reason.

It is not unthinkable that the pornographer is trying to say something—if not about his immediate subject, perhaps about society. It is easy to respond cynically to such a suggestion, but, after all, human beings often do express themselves in confused or repellent ways. It is the task of reason, when this happens, to penetrate confusion and overcome revulsion. But suppose nothing of communal value—nothing true and significant—is discovered. Reason still is not wholly silenced, for if confronted by pure pornography ("hardcore pornography") it can argue against pornography itself. Pornography may brush reason aside at the moment of impact, but reason can always wait. The sensations produced by pornography are notoriously unstable, and it is commonly reported that prolonged exposure to pornography leads to boredom. A patient reason may in some instances be better able to contend with lust, in its denial of personal dignity, by tolerating pornography than by suppressing it. In the latter situation, we may confront what D. H. Lawrence referred to as "the dirty little secret"—and that is perhaps more insidious and destructive than open obscenity.

If radicals typically wish to censor racism, and conservatives pornography, it is perhaps liberals who are most concerned about the vulgarity and violence often present in television programs. Here we face, as with pornography, an assault on personal dignity and on the possibility of communication. Is not common sense, however, already formulating a response that defends reason and communication without resorting to suppression? That response is to use public subsidies for destroying the monopoly of the commercial networks and the advertisers and to affirm man's dignity by initiating programs that appeal to his intelligence. The response to an assault on communication is thus found in the reassertion of communication. Reason is defended by reason itself, rather than by force.

It may be asked whether the standard of tolerance requires

openness toward every absurdity someone happens to express. It seems to me that the answer is: Yes, so far as there is time. Since we are mortal and finite, we cannot exhaustively consider every possible truth. We have to be guided by plausibility. But it would be well for us not to trust our sense of plausibility unreservedly. We cannot infallibly, at a glance, identify absurdities, and what strikes us as highly implausible may nevertheless be true. In Chapter Two, I argued that we have no right to believe things that are internally contradictory or in conflict with incontestable evidence. Where these conditions prevail, then, openness need be only temporary. But, even in the case of assertions that can be invalidated logically or empirically, there should be at least provisional openness—so long as there is time.

The attentive and open aspect of a tolerant society is not sufficiently indicated, however, merely by speaking of the need for tolerance. There is a need for liberty as well. More specifically, liberty of expression requires liberty of action. Tolerance has a boundless quality that makes it impossible to reduce it to permissiveness only where speech and the arts are concerned. One reason for this is that there is no clear and firm distinction between expression and action.

In principle, of course, there is such a distinction; it was sketchily introduced near the beginning of this essay. Expression as such—*pure* expression, like a Mozart symphony—aims only at placing certain contents of one mind before other minds (although developing the contents and expressing them must be a single event). Pure action, on the other hand, is directed toward preconceived, observable results, regardless of what enters into the minds of others. If most works of art are purely expressive, most crimes (not all) are probably purely active; far from trying to express anything, the criminal wishes his act to remain unknown.

Despite the clarity of the theoretical distinction, however, and despite its partial applicability, expression and action both are implicated to such a degree in most human undertakings that it is impossible to call those undertakings one or the other. For one thing, most serious expression influences action, even though that may not be its intention. Undoubtedly, Cézanne's painting, to consider one example, has affected our actions—although it would be impossible to specify exactly how—for it has affected the manner in which we see and imagine physical reality; the middle-class

Parisians who feared such painting may have held paltry and stuffy social ideals, but it was not foolish of them to feel threatened by the aesthetic revolution Cézanne represented.

Further, many expressions are formulated through action, and many actions are at the same time expressive. In other words, many of the things men do have a double intent—that of influencing other minds and that of accomplishing specific, observable results. A public demonstration, for example, is in some part a pure expression of feeling; but it is also directed at producing certain results. Almost every major act of a prominent public figure, such as an American president, has a double intent. And, even in our personal lives, much that we do is simultaneously an effort to express ourselves and to accomplish some result; clothes, houses, and automobiles are almost always instruments of both expression and action.

Finally, these two kinds of behavior are intermixed in the sense that all actions can be treated as expressions. For example, it is commonly assumed that almost every act of a great man is worthy of attention because of what it reveals about his mind. Psychoanalysis has found expressive significance in acts which seem altogether trivial. In a way, a biographer renders the whole life of his subject expressive, as a psychoanalyst does the whole life of a patient.

Since much that we do is indistinguishably expressive and active, tolerance cannot be confined to expression as distinguished from action. It cannot be argued that, so long as men are allowed to *say* whatever they like, it does not matter how extensively they are regulated in terms of what they *do*, for serious and effective saying is apt to be, in one way or another, a kind of doing, and most doing is some kind of saying. In short, freedom of expression would be severely limited if it were confined to what is *purely* expressive.

Even if expression and action were completely distinct, however, freedom of expression still would require liberality, the reason for this being simply that expression is emasculated if wholly severed from action. Thought and speech without practical application are apt to lead into a world of dreams and impossible demands. The extremism and willfulness so common in Russian political thought, and noticeably affecting minds even as great as those of Dostoevsky and Tolstoy, may be due largely to the forced separation of individual thought from political practice. A situation in which one can speak but not act invites intellectual corruption by removing the discipline of reality.

Liberality is bound to be misunderstood, however, if we equate freedom with governmental non-interference. Most workers of the nineteenth century were not free, although they were not enslaved. Blacks in America did not become free, nor did serfs in Russia, merely by being emancipated. A person is not free if he is unemployed or if he is employed for sixteen hours every day; he is not free if he is excluded from the institutions and facilities of the society around him; he is not free, except in a purely formal way, if he is uneducated or psychotic. Thus liberality is not an inevitable result of political passivity but rather the source of complex and exacting policy demands.

Tolerance asks more of society than the utmost freedom of expression, however, even though this is no slight or simple demand. There must be some rules, and tolerance asks that those rules be laid down only by the people, or by their representatives. Why? Because in this way not only are expression and action linked, but people are also impelled to come together in deliberation and decision. Tolerance is fully serious and fully communal only if it has consequences for the forms and powers of society, and these must be consequences deriving from the persuasive powers of those who are tolerated.

DEMOCRACY

The demos not only is often wrong; it is also often intolerant. There is little reason to think that majorities are usually wiser, or more attentive and open, than various minorities. The arguments for democracy that derive from the principle of tolerance are independent of these considerations. The central ideal on which they turn is that of comprehensiveness. The scope of tolerance ought to be as nearly universal as possible, judged in terms both of the persons and the subjects tolerated. The ideal is that of comprehensive attentiveness and openness—disciplined by involvement in action. The argument for democracy is that such comprehensiveness is not likely to be realized unless everyone shares in power.

In other words, the advantage of majority rule is that it maximizes persuasive efforts. Arrangements vesting the power of decision in majorities do not necessarily lead to correct decisions, but they must ordinarily cause political speech to be addressed to as many as can be reached. In this way the sphere of communication, and of communal tolerance, is widened to the utmost. This principle, of course, might need modification in view of special circumstances, such as the existence of an alienated minority, which would always be ignored under straight majority rule. However, barring such circumstances (which are perhaps uncommon, as the history of blacks in America might suggest), majority rule is a force on the side of universal communication.

The ideal we are concerned with, then, is only secondarily that of power in the hands of the people; it is primarily that of all-inclusive discourse, or at least all-inclusive tolerance. This is something fundamentally different from the collective absolutism that defines democracy for some of its proponents, such as Rousseau. The concept of democracy as all-inclusive discourse does not necessarily manifest great respect for the populace as a body; it does manifest respect for every person, along with skepticism concerning all powers and all ideologies.

An ideal of this kind necessarily entails a good deal more than votes for all. A tolerance that is widely inclusive and politically significant is bound to seek for everyone the opportunity—the question of whether or not everyone has the will and capacity aside—for a good liberal education. (The very purpose of a liberal education can be defined as that of cultivating attentiveness and openness.) Such a tolerance is bound also to seek a distribution of wealth wealth equitable enough to assure everyone the time and independence needed for taking part in public discussion. Meeting this minimum does not necessarily satisfy the requirements of justice, but it does create a situation in which all can take part in defining what the requirements of justice are.

The doors of public discourse ought to be repeatedly opened to the outcasts and the oppressed. Not only do such groups sometimes escape the pride and complacency usually affecting those thoroughly integrated with the established society; they often challenge an absolutized conception of man that is embodied in the existing society. Thus the claims of an underprivileged class or a despised race may liberate our sense of the human from confinement by unexamined dogmas concerning the nature of humanity. There is at least this much truth in the Marxist faith in the saving power of the proletariat.

The standard of comprehensiveness pertains not only to the downtrodden but also to the privileged. Marcuse urges that privileged groups be treated with deliberate intolerance. Perhaps in some instances they should be. It seems to me that what is needed fundamentally, however, is something very different from intolerance, namely, publicity. The privileged should be not merely tolerated but compelled to enter the public realm and to defend themselves rationally in terms of the public good. Assuming that they cannot be induced to do this voluntarily, then it must be done by their opponents, through exposure and analysis. Here radical scholars can play an important part in public life. It is, however, a part that demands abstinence from propaganda and an unshakable determination that nothing shall be left outside the purview of reason.

These reflections can serve to remind us that the ideal of democratic comprehensiveness is more easily defined than achieved. While the remedy Marcuse prescribes is dubious, the disease it is intended to cure is almost certainly real; tolerance in America lacks proper significance. The causes are manifold: a political order dependent on the contributions of the wealthy; a party system that necessarily blurs issues; a fragmentation of power that makes it often possible for power to be held and used outside the scope of public supervision; information media that do not effectively inform but rather entertain and distract; and academic social science that is quantitative and "value free" and thus ineffective in social criticism. Owing to these conditions, and to others, America is not as democratic in fact as it is in principle.

If we are concerned above all with tolerance, however, we must resist the conclusion that comprehensive tolerance would be assured merely if these obstacles to democracy were removed. Tocqueville, Mill, and a number of others whose observations cannot be casually discounted have found democracy itself intolerant and have seen an empowered populace as a censor of unparalleled effectiveness. It appears that, while democracy is a condition of comprehensive tolerance, it may nevertheless bring the very opposite result. This must happen whenever the majority is regarded as infallible. Stated so baldly, it may seem that few people regard the majority in this way; I suggest, however, that a great many do so tacitly, finding it easy, if not profitable, to acquiesce in whatever the greatest number prefers. The result is that democracy becomes a system for establishing an absolute power, not for universalizing communication.

The problem, then, is to keep a system that logically maximizes persuasion from being perverted, either by undemocratic minorities or by an idolized majority. Appeal is often made to some kind of authority, either to discover and represent the true interests of the people or to restrain the people in behalf of transcendent values. Some look in the opposite direction: participatory democracy is often seen as a way of opening the public realm to minorities suppressed and silent within the giant structures of twentieth-century society. The truth is, surely, that there is no solution to the problem. To rely either on authority or on the assembled demos is fundamentally idolatrous; it must lead away from the goal we are seeking, toward intolerance. The problem does, however, lead us to add to the requirements of liberality and democracy a third and final implication of tolerance for the social order.

If there were a single reliable answer to the problem of voiceless and powerless minorities, whether they are repressed by other minorities or by majorities, it would be that the voiceless must gain voices and the powerless must find ways of forcing those with power to take them into account. Both the appeal to authority and the idea of participatory democracy call on someone else to represent the suppressed minorities, at least provisionally. It would be more realistic to look to the suppressed minorities to rise up and represent themselves. This has often happened, as the recent history of blacks in America illustrates.

In what kind of society has this development the best chance of occurring? In a democracy, certainly, but in a particular kind of democracy—in one where no central power controls access to the public realm, where in tradition and law there is room for diversity. That is, in a pluralistic democracy.

PLURALISM

1

The general idea that a plurality of powers, social groups, parties, and policies underlies freedom is commonplace. A plurality of powers, checking one another, helps to safeguard freedom; the vitality and diversity of groups expresses and nourishes freedom; the availability of more than one party and policy is a major condition of freedom.

There is elemental truth in all of this. The point I wish to make here, however, is slightly different, namely, that pluralism is favorable to communication and thus to a communal and inquiring tolerance. For there to be communication, people must not only be united with one another, as discussed earlier in this chapter; they must also be set apart from one another, for communication is an act of joining and thus presupposes separateness and diversity as well as bonds and similarities. Historical experience indicates, for example, that peoples with ready access to the sea (Athens, the Netherlands, England), and thus to the customs and outlooks of other nations, have tended to be more inquiring and tolerant than nations set off from other nations by barriers of land (Sparta, Germany, Russia).

Community is the positive goal of pluralism. Community, however, is a product of freedom and therefore is not assured by any institutional arrangement. Consequently, pluralism is joined by links of causal certainty only to a negative goal—to that of relativizing every institution, every ideology, every policy, indeed, every historical entity. To relativize something is to set it in relationship to something else in order to make clear that it is not absolute and unchallengeable; it must be weighed in the scales and questioned.

To speak of this as a negative goal, however, is not to imply that it is unimportant. On the contrary, it is the precondition of both communication and tolerance. If there is a program, an institution, or a philosophy, that is absolute and unchallengeable, man is necessarily reduced to silence. Unrestricted communication presupposes universal relativity among historical powers and institutions. Tolerance can prevail only where all can be questioned.

By virtue of its negativity, pluralism has a certain priority over all other political and social standards. This priority comes not from the value of diversity in itself but rather from the fact that pluralism implicitly recognizes the relativity of all historical arrangements. Thus, for example, it is a more unconditional imperative than is the principle of democracy. The principle of democracy may come into conflict with other legitimate principles of political and social life, such as freedom or honor. The priority of pluralism derives from its recognition of the inevitability of such conflicts and of the consequent irreducible diversity of political and social principles. It is in view of these considerations that we dwell on the negative goal of pluralism in concluding this chapter.

The main premise of pluralism, it may be said, is that the established forms and powers of society should be continually subject to criticism and to change. Not that the vulnerability of society and the limits of human energy and courage require no times of relaxation and stability. But criticism and change should be frequent and pervasive enough, so that there are no safe and sheltered areas. Society and the sovereign political powers tend continually to become objects of a regard so exaggerated and unconditional as to be idolatrous. The most extreme results of this tendency are visible in Fascist and Communist totalitarianism, but the tendency is present everywhere. In America it is manifest in the recurrent seizures of belligerent patriotism and in the increasingly monarchical ascendancy and isolation of the president. The consequences are seen not only in the atrocities of totalitarian governments but, in more humane nations, in the vulgarity and repressiveness of typical patriotism, and in the insensitivity of governments to ordinary human needs. Life would become suffocating, and communication impossible, if man's natural social and political idolatry were not checked. I suggest that an established society, therefore, ought always to be more or less on the defensive. Some examples will indicate both the range of man's absolutizing tendency and the consequent need for negation.

Policies and plans   The collectivization of agriculture in the Soviet Union exemplifies the elevation of a plan to an absolute, and the millions of lives taken in order to effect this plan indicate the inhumanity inherent in holding to such an absolute. Governments should have to keep their policies experimental and their plans tentative. This view accords neither with the conservative belief that governments should pursue no great ends nor with the typical radical willingness that governments should bring about vast reforms unhesitatingly and forcefully.

Institutions   Man has a strong desire to divinize an institution. He has done this, in turn, with the city-state, the Roman Empire, the Catholic Church, the nation-state, and the Communist Party. All have been (using the phrase Hobbes applied to the state) "mortal gods." Both the right and the left have had their own mortal gods. An authentic and unqualified tolerance, seeking limitless community and undogmatic truth, must stay free of every kind of institutional idolatry.

Ideologies   Man also wishes to live according to an all-inclusive, harmonious, and unchallengeable world-picture. Until recent times, such a picture was often provided by Christians who were willing to reduce some of the most compelling symbols of ultimate meaning to a system of literal theological statements. The ideologies of

our time are secular replacements for the Christian world-picture.
It has been argued that ideologies now are receding into the past.
If this does not mean that we are sinking into a mood of pragmatic
triviality, we should be grateful and make no effort to create new
ideologies. A serious civilization needs transparency of environment, and opportunities for seeking and communicating the truth.
The world-pictures we long for, however, whether religious or secular, necessarily envision men as objects with set places in a rational totality. Thus, even though such pictures may represent highly
benevolent motives—eternal salvation, or justice on earth—they depersonalize human beings and open the way to violence.

Evils   Men absolutize not only things they love but also things
they hate and fear. This is not surprising, for to identify some finite
nite, destructible entity as the source of all evil wonderfully simpli-
fies life and offers immense hope for the future. Anti-Semitism is
one of the most vulgar and catastrophic results of the longing to
find an evil absolute. On the other end of the political spectrum,
however, many who are more rational and humane than the typical
anti-Semite have fallen victim to the same longing by making capitalism, or the bourgeoisie, an evil absolute. As America has become
more and more troubled with world responsibilities and internal
disintegration, many have sought relief by tracing every problem
back to Communism. A communal and truth-seeking tolerance
would negate the absolutes of hatred and fear, as well as those of
veneration and love.

A tolerant society refuses to identify itself with any plans,
institutions, ideologies, or crusades. It is in this sense resolutely
uncommitted.

Although tolerance may in some circumstances have to be limited, there should be no unconditional limits—nothing should be
treated as inherently exempt from negation. There have, of course,
been societies (like France or Germany in the eighteenth century)
tolerant enough to permit religious and intellectual minorities to
voice their philosophical beliefs, yet not tolerant enough to permit
criticism of established society and the state. Such restricted tolerance is neither inconsequential, as the French Revolution shows,
nor valueless. But tolerance is mutilated insofar as the dominant
powers, with their supporting institutions and ideologies, are exempt from intellectual attack, whether this comes about through
forcible suppression or through some kind of inconspicuous

nullification such as radicals accuse "the Establishment" of effecting today. Tolerance fulfills its functions only if it entails exposure and possible change for all powers, social forms, and beliefs.

2

The application of this view to the sovereign, to the government in its supremacy, has important implications.

One of these is that no government, no historical institution or power, can claim unconditional obedience. If every historical power and every idea is subject to criticism, then obedience must always be reflective and conditional. Such an assertion is not anarchistic. It is not a denial that government may be legitimate, for one may grant a government the right to command without committing himself to obey regardless of what is commanded. It is merely a claim of personal autonomy. In view of the relativity of all institutions and powers, the demands they make are necessarily subject to rational examination.

Another implication of the pluralistic view of government is that public advocacy of disobedience should be tolerated whenever possible. If a person can rightfully reflect before obeying, and question what he is called upon to do, then surely he can do this dialogically. And if man is a communal being, it is his duty, on deciding that a certain demand does not warrant acquiescence, to communicate this decision. My remarks about social cohesion and the limits of tolerance at the beginning of this chapter will make it clear that I do not deny that a government might in some circumstances have to silence those advocating disobedience. But it is hard to see why such advocacy ought to be barred in principle.

The same may be said of advocacy of the overthrow of the government by violence: it should not be outlawed in principle. Again, this is not to deny the right of a government to defend itself—even, in cases of "clear and present danger," by limiting speech. But the common view that only the advocacy of peaceful change is permissible is more restrictive than at first glance it appears to be. Technically, of course, established provisions for constitutional change—say, in the American Constitution—may be used to change anything in a constitution, including the process of change itself. But realistically, there is apt to be a great deal that cannot be accomplished through established procedures. Hence when it is asserted that we should be open only to proposals for peaceful change, a caveat that is reasonable on its face turns out to put narrow limits on reason.

If the legitimacy of the state can lawfully be called into question, however, then it seems that manifestations of disrespect for the state must also be tolerated. These are often highly distasteful. Desecration of the flag, for example, is not likely to be a graceful or appealing act. But it is practically always an act of communication. To deny freedom for such an act, or even attention, is a refusal of a possible human relationship and of thought. The objection may be made that one who wishes to communicate and to further thought should express himself by means of rational speech rather than by means of an act calculated to provoke an emotional reaction. This is probably true, at least for most circumstances. But practically all of the arguments I have set forth in behalf of tolerance imply that we do not pick and choose among possible interlocutors on the basis of the degree to which they adhere to the proper forms of communication as we understand them. Not that the forms of communication are unimportant. But communal man cannot place a priori bounds on attentiveness and openness; he must be receptive to every possibility of communication.

These arguments may be vehemently disputed by some readers; advocacy of disobedience and revolution and desecration of national symbols are apt to arouse deep antagonism. But are they in most circumstances mortally threatening to society? It can be argued that ordinarily they are not even dangerous; they merely belong in the category of the outrageous. I argue in favor of tolerating them not with the sense that I am calling for something particularly perilous but only with the sense that even though such a policy is rejected by many people, it has great importance.

It has importance first as a gauge of the amplitude of our tolerance. We are not really attentive and open unless we are ready to reflect critically on the whole order of society. This we are not likely to do except when the legitimacy of the government and the Constitution are forcefully challenged. Thus advocacy of disobedience and revolution, and desecration of national symbols, are not extremes that one can hardly expect tolerance to encompass. Rather, they are just the sort of provocations to fundamental thought that serious tolerance should welcome.

As for the bad judgment and offensive manners often accompanying these provocations, surely it is a sign of our humanity that they do not cause us to close our minds. We place those who

challenge us on a higher level of rationality than they themselves
assume by asking what they are attempting to say and how they
can be reasonably answered. We manifest our humanity, in short,
by assuming the burden of tolerance.

There is a second reason why tolerating challenges to the entire
political order seems to me important. This reason concerns the
age-old problem of political obligation, the problem of how it can
be rightfully demanded of a human being that he set aside his own
freedom and judgment in deference to another human being—one
who happens to be an official of the state. How can any government be legitimate? How can coercion ever be justified? The ideal
of tolerance underscores these questions by bringing out the moral
primacy of personal veracity and responsibility and the relativity
of all institutions and powers. At the same time, however, the ideal
of tolerance suggests a solution.

Tolerance of questions directed at the legitimacy of the state
would seem to be the very condition of legitimacy. If questions of
legitimacy, including the advisability of violent revolution, cannot
be discussed, how can a state be freely accepted by its citizens?
And if it is not freely accepted by its citizens, how can it be legitimate? Thus, while some feel that limitless tolerance shakes the
foundations of the state, it can be argued that without limitless
tolerance those foundations cannot have moral validity.

A similar logic applies to the question of coercion. It is doubtful that an act of coercion can be justified unless tolerance is extended to criticisms of that act and, by implication, to calls for disobedience. How otherwise is free and reflective obedience possible?
And how can it be said that the one coerced is treated as a human
being if he is not allowed to speak in protest? Through comprehensive tolerance, force is subordinated to community and those subjected to force are recognized in their humanity.

3

Pluralism expresses an abiding mistrust of society. In setting society
against itself, it seeks basically to set man against society. The ideal
it poses is not harmonious order but fruitful conflict.

Society is bound to be occasionally intolerant. Society is inherently base in that it is inherently impersonal—a matter of general,
more or less unchanging rules, made and upheld primarily by a few.
The idea of a perfect society is a contradiction in terms if "perfect"

is meant to denote exact correspondence with the present needs of every person within it, for "society" denotes qualities contrary to this correspondence: generality, changelessness, inequality. It is perhaps scarcely necessary to add that societies rarely even come near to the degree of perfection that in principle is possible. Prevailing customs and laws are likely to be not only general, and thus imperfectly adapted to particular instances, but also contrary to the interests of large numbers; they are likely to be not merely sufficiently firm to provide calculability but also rigid and out-of-date; the established inequalities are almost certain to entail greater privileges on one side and more drastic deprivations on the other than are required by the necessities of social organization. Given these characteristics, intolerance, both necessary and gratuitous, is inevitable.

The conflict of tolerance and society is not a conflict between good and evil, however. This is partly because tolerance often, if not always, fails to be effectively communal and inquiring; it sometimes makes room for irresponsibility and destructiveness. To say this is only to reiterate my criticism of Locke's and Mill's historical optimism.

On the other side, society is rarely so evil that it deserves to be wholly destroyed. Most societies not only meet a number of needs but also provide at least some of the conditions of a communal and truth-seeking tolerance. Thus, for example, to allow all order, unity, and deference to be lost under an onslaught of irresponsible critics would be a suicidal kind of tolerance. Society ought to be on the defensive but not defenseless.

Hence negation cannot be envisioned here, as it is in the thought of Marcuse, as a temporary measure that in time will enable a full community to come into being. It is rather an ideal of continuing conflict, and even this is an ideal, as distinguished from an expectation. Tolerance is a narrow pathway. It leads between two chasms—that of anarchy on one side and social absolutism on the other. Societies cannot be expected to walk that pathway for long without falling off to one side or the other. Thus to ask merely that society hold together and accomplish its basic functions while subjecting itself ceaselessly to critical and searching judgment is to set a high standard.

To put this in terms of traditional political theory, the ideal is one of duality rather than of dialectical progression. Both of these imply conflict. The distinguishing quality of dialectical progression, as conceived by Hegel and Marx, is that conflict leads finally to comprehensive harmony. This is a momentous distinction. Although dialectical theory can be a critical instrument of considerable power, as a whole it is a disguised form of social idolatry: at last, society will elevate man to a state of perfect freedom. What I am urging in place of dialectical progression is the concept of a conflict which in the long run cannot be counted on to lead anywhere but which has value in the short run and in itself—in the community and truth which may be realized by one generation and lost by the next and which are inherent in some measure in the very conflict itself.

The objection may be raised that this is to make an ideal of disorder and instability. I do not wish to do that. Within the range of historical possibilities, however, the non-ideal may be best. For example, the British system of government is almost always praised as liberal, responsible, and effective (all of which it has been); it is frequently contrasted with the French system under the Third and Fourth Republics, which supposedly entailed unstable and irresponsible government. It is probably true that French governments in some ways failed seriously; certainly French politics was ordinarily nerve-racking and unpredictable. But, in my view (despite admiration for both the British people and their government), France has provided a more stimulating environment than has Britain; and this, I suspect, has something to do with the fact that in France communication had more serious political consequences than in Britain. Along these lines, it is possible to argue that in the final analysis the French have been better governed than the British.

Roughly similar observations can be made concerning Sparta and Athens. The cultural works of antiquity have come so much to the fore of historical attention, and Athens' superiority to Sparta is so striking in this realm, that most people assume that Athens was better governed. I think that it was—but only if judged by standards that might lead one to say today that France has been better governed than Britain. This is not to suggest that Spartan government, with its militaristic and totalitarian characteristics, can be favorably compared with British government. It was, however, widely admired in ancient Greece and was thought by many intelligent people to be far superior to the Athenian government, which, like that of France, lacked stability and a definite center of responsibility.

CONCLUSION

It may seem that the tolerant society thus sketched—careful of its cohesion, even to the extent of limiting tolerance, yet attentive, democratic, and pluralistic—is incomplete, somehow in need of rounding off. Incompleteness, or tentativeness, however, is precisely the quality I have intended to suggest. No society is a community and no institution speaks with absolute authority concerning the requirements of community; practically every major argument in this essay has led us in the direction of these conclusions. What they imply is that we must resist our desire for a complete, rounded-off social ideal. We must bear the discomfort of a world in which no social arrangements, not even merely theoretical arrangements, can be wholly trusted.

Although a tolerant society is not a community, however, it is perhaps as near to community as man can come. Mutual tolerance is more communal than a state of all-consuming patriotism or revolutionary fervor; it is more communal than the shared thoughtlessness that may be induced by ancient customs and habits. As tense and unsatisfactory as it may seem, a tolerant society is at least precariously ready for community. Human beings have often been further from community than that.

Toward a New Civility

ALTHOUGH THE STANDARD of tolerance does not point the way toward an ideal society, it does point the way toward selfhood—selfhood saved from the treacherous historical tides that are moving about us. Since, as Jesus asserted, the loss of selfhood nullifies every other gain, it is this aspect of tolerance that concerns us above all. More urgent than the question of the tolerant society is the question of the tolerant self. This has been the underlying subject of this essay all along; it is the purpose of these final few pages only to make this clear by drawing together, and sharpening the outlines of, some of the preceding arguments.

As a standard for personal life, tolerance prescribes a certain stance. This stance, I believe, is the one required of man if he is successfully to resist the destructive forces of history, yet not withdraw from history—to save himself, yet do this through a certain manner of involvement rather than through an attempt at total detachment. In short, the standard of tolerance indicates how we should relate ourselves to the life of our times; it teaches civility. What is the nature of this civility?

It is, first of all, a kind of standing clear. Tolerance requires autonomy. On its face, of course, tolerance is a refusal wholly to repudiate any manifestation of historical being, a refusal conclusively to suppress any communication. This may seem like something very different from autonomy—an acceptance of everything, all-inclusive acquiescence. The refusal to repudiate any manifestation of historical being, however, presupposes a refusal to identify oneself wholly with any such manifestation. It is possible to be tolerant only through being in some measure disengaged from every party, leader, and ideology. The tolerant stance, then, is one of personal independence. Here the note of saving oneself—by keeping apart—sounds strongly.

The autonomy required by tolerance does not imply isolation, however; it is fundamentally communal. Rather than being required by an aloof and regal self, it is required by the love of mankind and even, it may be said, by the love of universal being. One implicitly turns away from mankind and from being when he engages in an absolute historical commitment. To say this, of course, is to recur to the major themes of this essay. Man disposes himself toward the totality of things (a metaphorical expression) through attentiveness and openness. But every absolute historical commitment restricts the range of attentiveness and openness; there are people I will not hear and possible truths I cannot consider. This is why attentiveness and openness require autonomy.

On one side, this communality is illimitable, and thus opens out toward the unconditioned, or to what Buber called "the eternal Thou." This is not to say that any such reality is necessarily affirmed, but only that it cannot be denied a priori. This takes us back to a question briefly discussed earlier in the essay. The boundless quality of attentiveness and openness is manifest in a willingness to experience the "sense of eternity" that, as brought out in Chapter Three, may be logically presupposed by the standard of tolerance. On the other side, however, while attentiveness and openness orient man toward eternity, they also entail immediate and concrete relationships. One cannot be related to encompassing realities, such as mankind, if he is inattentive and closed toward the actual human beings whom he happens to encounter. The communality underlying autonomy is unreal unless it enters into the associations of daily life.

Moreover, the autonomy required by tolerance is not only communal; it is also active. For man to assume a stance of detached contemplation—one kind of autonomy—is to play at infinitude; no possibility is rejected, no particular position is taken. In this way, however, one abstracts himself not only from his actual, finite being but also from the human race. He tries to stand above the plurality of human existence, awash in finitude, and in this way he betrays communality. To be communal, a person must accept status as one individual among many; this in turn is to accept finitude, a condition requiring one to be a determinate being, excluding many possibilities and occupying a certain position—a condition accepted through choice and action. To put this in terms of the subject of this essay, one is genuinely and intelligently tolerant only by supporting the conditions of tolerance in actual historical situations, and this must always mean supporting certain leaders, parties, and programs.

Choice must always be tentative, however, or it would be incompatible with autonomy. Writers today often glorify "commitment," apparently thinking of choice that is unconditional and irrevocable.

This seems to me false, and moreover dangerous. Making irrevocable choices is another way of playing at infinitude, as though it were for man to be one in whom there is "no shadow of turning." In our actual finitude, we can never be sure that we have chosen rightly; to resolve our uncertainties through defying every temptation to reconsider is only to enter a willful darkness. The self, then, is to be found neither through pure detachment nor through pure commitment, but through alternation between choice and reconsideration. It necessarily follows that every political and ideological association must be provisional, subject to challenges that—coming from the self one is trying to save—cannot be ignored.

My emphasis on the communality and activity presupposed in autonomy have one central purpose: to show that the tolerant self is not an abstract, indeterminate center of negation. It is not a void created by non-involvement. It can be said that man in some sense *is* his relationships; all marks of identity—vocation, interests, place of residence—are relationships. The idea of a person without relationships is self-contradictory. This is recognized throughout the present essay. I have tried to develop a standard according to which tolerance is primarily a state of comprehensive relatedness—to persons and to truth; to "the eternal Thou" (as at least a possibility), to mankind, and to particular persons; through inquiry and through action. If man is his relationships, then the tolerant self, in its universal relatedness, seeks the fullest measure of concrete selfhood.

We can now see what I wish above all to bring out in these closing pages: that tolerance, as a form of relatedness, is also a certain way of caring for the self. How can this care be aptly denoted? What attitude toward the self is implied by autonomy, communality, and activity?

If these questions can be answered in a word, that word, I suggest, is "availability." To be tolerant is not only to let others come forth in their genuine being; it is also to let oneself thus come forth. The self is cared for by making it available. We often speak of "self-knowledge" or "self-possession." It is only things, and not persons, however, that I can know and possess; least of all can I *know* or *possess* the person I am. My relationship with myself is not wholly unlike my relationship with others: I become manifest, as one whom I do not fully know or control, through communication. To be available is to be related to others through receptivity to the manifestation of the self. The complexities of this attitude, arising from the insensitivity of others, the restraints of society, and legitimate considerations of shame and reserve, are vast, but they do not affect the essential idea of availability, namely, that one cultivates selfhood by making room for it, so to speak, between oneself and others, and that this is done through tolerance.

There is no difficulty in seeing why availability is required on the part of a tolerant person. As defined in this essay, tolerance invites others to manifest themselves freely, and it is based on man's communal nature, his essential solidarity with others. But this solidarity requires one to give expression to one's own being as well as inviting others to do so. In short, communication means mutuality.

It may seem, however, that it is rather late in the essay to introduce so novel a concept. This might well be true if the concept were really being introduced for the first time in the course of these reflections; but it is not, it summarizes an attitude already analyzed with care—that set forth in terms of veracity and responsibility. Both of these are aspects of availability, veracity being the availability of a cognitive being, responsibility that of an acting being. Hence what is said here takes us only a step beyond Chapter Two. To be tolerant, it is necessary to be veracious and responsible, as well to allow others to be so. Or, one who permits others to be available must be available himself. It is in responding to this necessity that one cultivates and guards his own being.

Tolerance may be regarded as a kind of hospitality—toward persons (attentiveness) and toward truth (openness). Through this hospitality, one creates an area of humanity, an area in which human beings can fulfill the urge to be united with one another and with being. While I am recapitulating here themes worked out earlier in the essay, what I am adding is the reminder that hospitality toward others logically entails hospitality toward oneself. I, too, must be prepared to enter the area of humanity.

We find ourselves drawing together some of the main threads in these reflections—attentiveness and openness, and veracity and responsibility. It is unnecessary to consider the correlations among these virtues (that through openness, for example, one checks his own veracity). What mainly matters to us here is that these virtues provide a general definition of civility—of the stance of a person who, as far as possible, relates himself (attentively and openly, veraciously and responsibly) to all mankind, yet makes these relations the substance of a resolutely critical and independent personality;

who stands apart and takes care above all of his own soul, yet bases this care on recognition that his being is not single and self-contained but consists in relationships.

Civility is a stance for all times, but it is perhaps one particularly suited to our own times. This is partly because it counters political despair. It rejects the temptation, arising powerfully from the tragedies of our time, to turn away from the world of mankind and to look for refuge in private life. It denies that the self can be saved by withdrawal, whatever the violence and senselessness reigning in history. What is more, it rejects the temptation, also arising powerfully from recent experiences, to sacrifice the self to a party, a leader, a political dogma, or some other idol. It is based on the Socratic-Christian conviction that an individual's primary responsibility is not for history but for the state of his own soul. This conviction expresses not indifference to history but rather a sense of the limits of an individual's wisdom and power. And it does not express indifference to human beings; on the contrary, the state of one's soul is seen as determined by the state of his relationships.

In summary, I am suggesting that tolerance shows us, when it is fully understood, how to bear ourselves in the trials of history; it defines the contours of civility. A person who is tolerant resists the temptations of judgment and violence. In doing this, he makes a space in which communal relationships are possible and in which, even if such relationships never materialize, he may himself survive in his humanity. A tolerant person creates a sanctuary for the self. This he does not directly intend; it is inherent in the universal hospitality that constitutes his tolerance.

Tolerance is a far less dramatic posture than those encouraged by the political ideologies that have been put forth up to now. Radicalism, for example, presents man with visions of imminent worldly paradise and instills certitude and determination. A tolerant person is skeptical and uneasy before these visions, and is unwilling to sever decision from doubt. Radicals often are convinced that they are carried forward by the fundamental forces of history, whereas a tolerant person feels that history is not only meaningful and sometimes liberating but also enigmatic and menacing.

On the other side, conservatives see a long-established political order like that of the United States as a refuge from the intellectual uncertainties, the moral errors, and the loneliness attacking man in the twentieth century; here one can be believing, righteous, and united with others. One who is lucidly and fully tolerant, however, must eschew the false comforts of this refuge without resorting to any other refuge.

It would be easy to say that for many to adopt so uncommitted and precarious a posture would set political affairs adrift and invite disaster. But perhaps this is not so. Beginning with the French Revolution in 1789, there have been several national efforts to reach perfect justice by will and design. The results have tended always toward dictatorship and terror. Americans have hardly been less proud and confident than the revolutionaries of France, Russia, and China, even though they have not tried to fashion an earthly paradise by means of the power of the state; they have differed from them mainly in mistrusting government and relying instead on private genius and natural historical progress. The results have been not dictatorship and terror but a strong and pervasive sense that affairs are out of control and contain deadly potentialities. The tragedies of recent history are ironical, as Reinhold Niebuhr so powerfully argued, in that they are drastically incongruous with the hopes and plans that preceded them, yet in some part they have been caused by the very heedlessness of those hopes and plans. Perhaps, then, by respecting the mystery of things, we shall rediscover a harmony lost through the willfulness of revolutionaries and industrial entrepreneurs. Perhaps by seeking less we shall achieve more. That would be no more ironical than the fact that by seeking a great deal we seem to have come near to losing everything.

But tolerance is mainly to be recommended not for its consequences, since a realistic tolerance must acknowledge that these are uncertain, but for its inherent fitness. It is truer to the obscure and trying character of reality and the limitations of men than are the ideologies. Above all, it is truer to man's supreme responsibility, that of keeping himself facing in the direction of humanity and truth in times that invite one to despair of everything but immediate pleasure. Tolerance is the practice of this fidelity; it is a readiness (borrowing a phrase from Saint Paul) for speaking and hearing "the truth in love." [3] One who maintains himself in a state of such readiness will probably not save mankind and the world but at least he will see to what is his main concern—his own communal and truthful bearing in an age of tribulation and despair.

NOTES

INTRODUCTION

1 John Stuart Mill, *Utilitarianism, Liberty, and Representative Government*, introd. by A. D. Lindsay (New York: E. P. Dutton & Co., 1951), p. 93.

I TOLERANCE AND THE LIBERAL FAITH

1 John Locke, *On Politics and Education*, ed. with an introd. by Howard Penniman (New York: D. Van Nostrand, 1947), p. 37.

2 Ibid., p. 53.

3 Mill, op. cit., p. 99. The italics are Mill's.

4 Matthew 7:14.

5 Locke, op. cit., p. 38.

6 Ibid., p. 53.

7 Mill, op. cit., p. 98.

8 Ibid., p. 96.

9 Locke, op. cit., p. 53.

10 Ibid., p. 32.

11 Ibid., pp. 51-52.

12 Locke, op. cit., p. 52.

13 Mill, op. cit., p. 109.

14 Abrams vs. United States. 250 U. S. 616, 1919.

15 Mill, op. cit., p. 138.

16 Ibid., p. 127.

17 Ibid., p. 108. Actually he asks *why* there is such a preponderance, but the question is rhetorical.

18 Robert Paul Wolff, Barrington Moore, Jr., and Herbert Marcuse, *A Critique of Pure Tolerance* (Boston: Beacon Press, 1965).

19 See, for example, Etienne Gilson, *The Christian Philosophy of St. Thomas Aquinas*, trans. by L. K. Shook (New York: Random House, 1956).

20 Mill, op. cit., pp. 137-138.

21 Locke, op. cit., p. 33.

22   Mill, op. cit., p. 104.

23   Ibid., p. 105.

24   Locke, op. cit., p. 61.

25   Mill, op. cit., p. 171.

26   Thomas Hobbes, *Leviathan*, ed. with an introd. by Michael Oakeshott (Oxford: Basil Blackwell, n.d.), p. 6.

27   Ibid.

28   Georg Wilhelm Friedrich Hegel, *The Philosophy of History*, with prefaces by Charles Hegel and the translator, J. Sibree, rev. ed. (New York: Willey Book Co., 1900), p. 20. The italics are Hegel's.

29   Ibid., p. 21.

II   WHY SHOULD MEN BE TOLERANT?

1   Mill, op. cit., p. 126.

2   See *Lectures on the Principles of Political Obligation*, with an introd. by Lord Lindsay of Birker (New York: Longmans, Green & Co., 1941).

3   This aspect of Rousseau's thought is brought out strongly in his *Considérations sur le gouvernement de Pologne*, in *The Political Writings of Jean Jacques Rousseau*, ed. by C. E. Vaughan (New York: John Wiley & Sons, 1962), Vol. II.

4   See Jean Jacques Rousseau, *The Social Contract and Discourses*, trans. with an introd. by G. D. H. Cole (New York: E. P. Dutton & Co., 1950), pp. 127-141.

5   See Ferdinand Tönnies, *Community and Society*, trans. and ed. by Charles P. Loomis (New York: Harper & Row, 1957).

6   Ibid., p. 33.

7   Ibid., p. 34.

8   This principle has been very effectively argued by T. H. Green.

9   This is exemplified by the controversy created by Hannah Arendt's book on Eichmann. See Hannah Arendt, *Eichmann in Jerusalem: A Report on the Banality of Evil*, rev. and enl. ed. (New York: Viking Press, 1963), where the author suggests, as the subtitle indicates, that Eichmann was thoughtlessly ordinary rather than fanatical.

10   Herbert Marcuse, *An Essay on Liberation* (Boston: Beacon Press, 1969), p. 26.

11   Søren Kierkegaard, *Philosophical Fragments, or A Fragment of Philosophy*, trans. by David Swenson; trans. rev. by Howard V. Hong (Princeton, N. J.: Princeton University Press, 1936), p. 46.